What's Next?

A Simulation of Adult Life Stages

Heidi Retzer and Dan Heisdorf

WALCH EDUCATION

1   2   3   4   5   6   7   8   9   10

ISBN 978-0-8251-6468-2

Copyright © 2008

J. Weston Walch, Publisher

40 Walch Drive • Portland, ME 04103

www.walch.com

Printed in the United States of America

Table of Contents

Part 1

Playing
What's Next?

Introduction

What's Next? is a simulation of life. This simulation game is designed to represent a model of four different stages of adulthood: You Are Done with High School, Living on Your Own, You Are Married, and You Have a Family. The role-play activities encourage students to learn the skills they will need to make the transition into adulthood. *What's Next?* is structured so students gain and practice money management, decision making, critical thinking, and life skills as they participate in a game-like activity. It is designed to be used in combination with a life-skills curriculum or a consumer mathematics curriculum, but it can be combined with most curricula. In addition, the model activities can be used as a classroom management program, because as students progress through the simulation, class attendance and performance earns money for the student.

The exercises can be used with all middle- and high-school age students preparing for post-secondary life. The activities meet the national standards for No Child Left Behind. They also help address federal special education laws for Individual Education Plans that require transition to be considered for students at the age of 14, and met for students at the age of 16.

Teacher Overview

What's Next? allows students to experience the financial responsibilities they will have as adults, while teaching them the skills they need to be more successful in this aspect of adult life. The simulation begins by engaging students in the world of earnings. Students are no longer just students—they are working citizens. In the first stage, You Are Done with High School, the student's job is to come to class to earn "money." Students (or workers) will earn "money" by being punctual workers who generate quality work. Students will be paid when they complete a time sheet, which will provide their employer (the teacher) with the information needed to write them a weekly paycheck. Each student is responsible for keeping his or her time sheet on a daily basis, as many workers are required to do.

Just as in real life, as responsibilities change and life becomes more costly, the simulation changes, too. Starting with the second stage, Living On Your Own, students also need to deduct taxes from their pay. During the third stage, You Are Married, students must consider health insurance. After students are paid, they must also face the financial responsibility of paying their bills, which is part of every adult's life.

As students progress through the simulation, they will find that the number and amount of their bills will increase significantly. Some events that happen in life are beyond one's control. To replicate this, the game incorporates life's "perks and pitfalls." The unforeseen events illustrate life's financial ups and downs. At the end of the week, each student will write the appropriate checks and deposit tickets, and record them in a checkbook register.

Implementing *What's Next?*

Time Required

What's Next? is flexible; there is no set amount of time for implementing the program. You can use the entire program to simulate each of the four phases of adulthood, or each phase of adulthood can be used on its own for the length of time that fits students' needs. Each simulated stage of a person's adult life fits easily into a quarter of the school year (approximately 40 class sessions). The activities within each stage of life will take between 30 to 60 minutes of the student's time. The time varies depending on the activity and the thoroughness required. The activities can be completed in class or assigned as homework.

Getting Started: Preparing and Organizing Yourself

In this book, you will find explicit implementation instructions for running the simulation, student instructions for each stage, the necessary financial record keeping tools, and other materials to simulate life as an adult. At the beginning of each stage, the setup takes some planning. Each stage includes a list of the supplies necessary to complete this simulation, and you will find that most of the materials are common and easy to find. Preparing the simulation will require you to photocopy, laminate, and organize the component activities in folders, and make individual handouts available when the implementation instructions indicate. The simulation also requires each student to have a folder or a binder to organize his or her materials. It is up to you to decide whether to provide the folders or binders, or require students to provide their own.

Once the initial setup is complete, you will act as a facilitator for *What's Next?* As an employer oversees the workers, you will be making sure employees show up for work on time, inform them when they complete quality work, monitor the completion of the worker's time sheets, and write out weekly paychecks. However, unlike an employer, you will be assisting your students in meeting their financial obligations by monitoring their payment of bills and the accuracy of their financial record keeping. Therefore, if you have successfully held a job and completed your financial obligations as an adult, you are equipped with all of the background knowledge you need to act as a facilitator for *What's Next?* Keep in mind, what is common sense to an adult is new uncharted territory for many pre-teens and teenagers.

Getting Started: Preparing and Organizing Students

Prior to starting *What's Next?* it is important for students and their parents or guardians to understand they will be participating in a simulation game. You may provide this information as an invitation to each of your students (provided on page 4). With this invitation, you should provide the "*What's Next?* Student Overview." Review this information with your students, and encourage them to share this information with their parents or guardians.

During each of the stages, students will be asked to investigate several areas adults must consider, individually or with a partner. Parents or guardians will become involved when their child consults them about their expertise in handling the financial obligations of life. This real-world research will help students understand that adult decisions can be difficult to make.

In general, the grouping to be utilized in the simulation will allow students to assist one another and to learn from one another's unique perspectives. During the simulation, students will primarily make individual decisions. However, to assist each student and to check for accuracy in keeping his or her time card and completing his or her other financial obligations, consider pairing students. Students may select their own partner, you can assign partners, or the partners can be selected randomly. Initially, gender will not be a factor when pairing students, but if you would like to have the same partners during all four stages of the simulation, partners should be of the opposite gender when possible. During the You Are Married and You Have a Family stages, students will be asked to work with a partner of the opposite gender to complete the additional financial consideration activities. If there are not an equal number of males and females in the class, groups of three can be utilized.

Name _____ Date _____

You Are Invited!

Have you ever daydreamed about what life as an adult will be like? Well, you will be able to experience life as an adult because you have been invited to participate in a simulation game called *What's Next?* This simulation will occur during

_____.

      (name of class and time)

This simulation allows you to experience life as an adult prior to actually having to live it. *What's Next?* will provide you with the experience to learn about an adult's ability to earn money and the financial obligations that go with adulthood. To further understand the simulation, read the Student Overview.

As part of the simulation, you will also be asked to investigate and give careful consideration to aspects of an adult's life that you may have never thought about. You will investigate the different areas on your own or with a partner. As you investigate, you will be asked to use a variety of resources, but the best resources are adults such as your parents or guardians. Therefore, it is important to let your parents know about the *What's Next?* simulation. To help you explain it to them, use your Student Overview sheet as a guide.

Your signature and the signature of a parent or guardian acknowledge that you have received this exciting invitation. This is an invitation to experience "life," to learn some important lessons, and to guide you as you grow into a responsible adult.

_____   _____
Student signature   Parent or guardian signature

Name _____ Date _____

Student Overview

What's Next? is a game you will be playing to help you gain and practice money management and decision-making skills that you will need as an adult. As you participate in the game, you will be "paid" to attend this class and complete quality class work. After completing a time card, you will receive a paycheck each week, which you will deposit in to your *What's Next?* bank account. As you progress through the game, you will learn what type of bills and tax responsibilities you might have as an adult. For your bills, you will need to write out checks, and for your tax responsibilities, you will be adjusting your total gross pay. Basically, the game will allow you to earn money, but it will also show you what your future financial responsibilities might be.

You can't always plan for certain events in life. In the game, these unplanned events are called the "perks" and "pitfalls" of life. Each week, you will be asked to select one of the two. Sometimes you will select a perk that helps you financially, but sometimes a pitfall will hurt you financially.

The money you earn will be tabulated on a weekly basis. To succeed in this game, you will need to make good personal and financial decisions, but there will also be luck involved. As in life, your goal is to make enough money to pay your expenses, but you may also want to have money on reserve for a "rainy" day expense or to purchase a luxury item in the future. This money can earn you points towards your grade or other incentives as determined by your teacher.

Enjoy the game, and good luck finding out *"What's Next?"*

Mid-Contintent Research for Education and Learning (McRel) Standards Correlations

Family/Consumer Sciences: Resources Management

Standard 4: Understand how knowledge and skills related to consumer and resources management affect the well-being of individuals, families and society.

What's Next? **Activities:**

- Use of loan agreement; completion of post-secondary commitment sheet and fixed expense sheet; understanding of revolving bills and financial perks and pitfalls; completion of What I Need to Know About Health Insurance, Renting, Purchasing a Car, Opening a Checking Account, Comparing Credit Cards, Buying Appliances, Your Food Allowance, Furnishing a Place to Live, Savings, Buying a House, Having a Baby, Child Care, Family Vacations and Saving for Your Child's Education, Pets

Family/Consumer Sciences: Family Life

Standard 2: Understand the impact of the family on the well-being of individuals and society.

What's Next? **Activities:**

- Are Men and Women Really That Different?, Buying a House, Celebrations, Family Vacations, Having a Baby, Having a Baby, Raising Your Children, Child Care

Family/Consumer Sciences: Living Environments

Standard 6: Understand how knowledge and skills related to living environments affect the well-being of individuals, families, and society.

What's Next? **Activities:**

- Rent, House Payments, Living with a Roommate, Renting, Utility Bills, Furnishing a Place to Live, Buying Appliances, Buying a House, Perks and Pitfalls

Family/Consumer Sciences: Child Development

Standard 10: Understands how knowledge and skills related to child development affect the well being of individuals, families, and society.

What's Next? **Activities:**

- Having a Baby, Raising Your Children, and Child Care

Life Skills: Life Work

Standard 3: Manages money effectively.

What's Next? **Activities:**

- Completion of financial records (checks, deposit tickets, and check register); paying of weekly bills; participation in *What's Next?* Auction, Completion of Your Food Allowance, Furnishing a Place to Live, and Entertainment Allowance

Standard 6: Makes effective use of basic life skills.

What's Next? **Activities:**

- Completion of weekly time sheet; completion of financial records; completion of Taxes: They Never Go Away, W-4 form, and What I Need to Know About Health Insurance

Standard 7: Displays reliability and a basic work ethic.

What's Next? **Activities:**

- Completion of weekly time sheet

Life Skills: Working with Others

Standard 4: Displays effective interpersonal communication skills.

What's Next? **Activities:**

- Completion of Are Men and Women Really That Different?, Buying a House, Family Vacation, Celebrations, Having a Baby, Raising Your Children, Child Care, and Pets

Name _____ Date _____

Weekly Time Sheet

For the week of _____

Name _____	Volunteering points _____
Date _____	Project points _____
Attendance points _____	Miscellaneous points _____
Assignment points _____	Gross pay _____
Name _____	Volunteering points _____
Date _____	Project points _____
Attendance points _____	Miscellaneous points _____
Assignment points _____	Gross pay _____
Name _____	Volunteering points _____
Date _____	Project points _____
Attendance points _____	Miscellaneous points _____
Assignment points _____	Gross pay _____
Name _____	Volunteering points _____
Date _____	Project points _____
Attendance points _____	Miscellaneous points _____
Assignment points _____	Gross pay _____
Name _____	Volunteering points _____
Date _____	Project points _____
Attendance points _____	Miscellaneous points _____
Assignment points _____	Gross pay _____

Name _____ Date _____

Total gross pay _____	Health insurance _____
FICA (6.2%) _____	Miscellaneous deductions _____
Medicare (1.45%) _____	
Federal income tax _____	
State tax (optional) _____	Total take-home pay _____

_____ 20 _____ 71-587/749

PAY TO THE
ORDER OF _____ $ _____

_____ DOLLARS

FIRST NATIONAL BANK

FOR _____ _____

⑆074905872⑆ 251⑈372⑈8⑈ 4311

Checks

	20 _____ 71-587/749

PAY TO THE
ORDER OF _____ $ _____

_____ DOLLARS

FIRST NATIONAL BANK

FOR _____

⑈074905872⑈   251⑈372⑈8⑈ 4311

---

	20 _____ 71-587/749

PAY TO THE
ORDER OF _____ $ _____

_____ DOLLARS

FIRST NATIONAL BANK

FOR _____

⑈074905872⑈   251⑈372⑈8⑈ 4311

---

	20 _____ 71-587/749

PAY TO THE
ORDER OF _____ $ _____

_____ DOLLARS

FIRST NATIONAL BANK

FOR _____

⑈074905872⑈   251⑈372⑈8⑈ 4311

Deposit Tickets

CASH _____ _____

CHECK _____ _____

CHECK _____ _____

TOTAL FROM OTHER SIDE _____ _____

SUB TOTAL _____ _____

LESS CASH _____ _____

NET DEPOSIT _____ _____

DATE _____

SIGNATURE _____

FIRST NATIONAL BANK

⑆074905872⑆   251⑈372⑈8⑈ 4311

CASH _____ _____

CHECK _____ _____

CHECK _____ _____

TOTAL FROM OTHER SIDE _____ _____

SUB TOTAL _____ _____

LESS CASH _____ _____

NET DEPOSIT _____ _____

DATE _____

SIGNATURE _____

FIRST NATIONAL BANK

⑆074905872⑆   251⑈372⑈8⑈ 4311

CASH _____ _____

CHECK _____ _____

CHECK _____ _____

TOTAL FROM OTHER SIDE _____ _____

SUB TOTAL _____ _____

LESS CASH _____ _____

NET DEPOSIT _____ _____

DATE _____

SIGNATURE _____

FIRST NATIONAL BANK

⑆074905872⑆   251⑈372⑈8⑈ 4311

Check Register

RECORD ALL CHARGES OR CREDITS THAT AFFECT YOUR ACCOUNT

NUMBER	DATE	DESCRIPTION OF TRANSACTION	PAYMENT/DEBIT (–)	√ T	FEE (IF ANY)	DEPOSIT/CREDIT (+)	BALANCE $	

Name _____ Date _____

What Are Your Fixed Expenses?

Use this page to record important information about your bills, marital status, children, and more.

Name _____

Current stage _____

Post-secondary education decision _____

Single/married/divorced _____

Spouse's income _____

Withholding allowance _____

Loan payment (if any) _____

Payee _____

Housing (rural or urban) _____

Housing (rent or house payment) _____

Landlord/holder of mortgage _____

Cell phone provider _____

Auto loan payment (1) _____

Payee for auto loan (1) _____

Auto loan payment (2) _____

Payee for auto loan (2) _____

Health insurance premium _____

Number of children _____

Age of children _____

Child care expenses _____

Loan Agreement Description

The loan agreement is an optional piece of paperwork, and it is left to your discretion whether or not it will be used. There may be times during the game when a student overdraws his or her account, especially if he or she has a pitfall that is financially devastating. If you decide not to use the loan agreement, the student who is unable to pay his or her bills will continue to financially "dig a hole." The student will continue to overdraw his or her account as the bills pile up. If you decide to use the loan agreement, the loan can be made between students, or between a student and you. The student loaning the money must have enough in his or her account to cover the loan. Those involved can determine the interest rate for the loan, and can make a schedule to pay it back. However, the loan agreement clearly delineates the loan agreement and the payment schedule, so there is no confusion about the loan. If the loan is between students, the lender will write out a check, and the borrower will deposit the check. Thereafter, the borrower will write out a check on the predetermined payment schedule. If one student is lending to another, both students should keep a copy of the loan agreement. If the loan is between a student and you, the teacher, the student will write out a check to you on the predetermined payment schedule. Both you and the student should have a copy of the loan agreement.

Name _____ **Date** _____

Loan Agreement

I, _____, agree to pay back _____,
(person) the amount of $_____, which was loaned on
_____ (date). I agree to pay back $ _____ on a
_____ basis. We have agreed upon _____% interest, which will
be calculated on a _____ basis.

Below is the payment schedule:

I, _____, agree if I default on the loan _____
has the right/privilege to file a claim in _____ Court of Law.

_____   _____
Signature of loan applicant   Date

_____   _____
Signature of lender   Date

_____   _____
Signature of teacher   Date

Name _____ Date _____

What You Need to Remember When Dealing with Bank Transactions

❏ your pay stub

❏ your pitfall or perk

❏ which bills are due

Name _____ Date _____

Weekly Reminder Sheet

This week, don't forget . . .

_____

_____

_____

_____

_____

_____

_____

_____

_____

_____

_____

_____

_____

_____

_____

_____

_____

_____

_____

_____

Name _____ Date _____

Completing Paperwork

Use the following information to complete your paperwork.

Your Time Sheet

1. Fill in the time period for this time sheet.

2. Do not fill out the check—your teacher will complete this at the end of the week.

3. Fill in your complete name. If you do not fill this in, your teacher will not know who to pay, and you might not get paid.

4. Fill in each date.

5. Fill in your attendance points on a daily basis—if you were late or did not call in, you need to put in negative points and have your teacher initial it.

6. Fill in assignment, volunteering, project, and miscellaneous points the day they are given.

7. Total your gross pay on a daily basis.

8. Add the daily totals to calculate the total gross pay.

9. To start the second stage of the game, calculate the taxes you owe, and subtract from the total gross pay to determine your total take-home pay.

10. Turn in your completed pay stub to the predetermined spot by the deadline.

Name _____ Date _____

Your Checks

On a weekly basis, you will need to write out a check for your bills and other expenses.

1. When you write out the check, write in ink.

2. Fill in the correct date on the check.

3. Complete the "Pay to the order of" line. Be sure to use an actual name—not descriptions or nicknames.

4. Write the amount of the check in numerals in the box and in words on the blank below the "Pay to the order of" line.

5. Sign your legal name on the line at the bottom right of the check.

6. You can indicate what the check is for in the "For" line.

Your Deposit Tickets

On a weekly basis, you will need to deposit the money you earned or received into the bank. To assist yourself and the bank teller in organizing your deposit, you will need to complete a deposit ticket.

1. When you write out the deposit ticket, write in ink.

2. Fill in the correct date on the deposit ticket.

3. In the spot allocated for cash, write the amount of cash you wish to deposit.

4. In the spot allocated for checks, write in the amount of each of the checks. If you have more deposits than the space provided, list them on the back of the deposit slip.

5. Add the totals of each of the checks to determine a subtotal.

Name _____ Date _____

6. If you want cash returned to you, you would list this amount on the "less cash" line. Do this only if your teacher instructs you to do so.

7. Subtract the less cash from the subtotal amount to determine the net deposit.

8. Sign your name on the deposit ticket.

Your Check Register

After you have written the checks and deposit tickets, keep a record of the transactions in your check register.

1. For a deposit, write the date of the deposit, write the word *deposit* under "description of transaction," and write the total amount in the correct column. After you write in the amount, add the deposit amount to the previous balance.

2. For a check, write the date of the check, write the name of the person or business you wrote the check to under "description of transaction," and write the amount in the correct column. After you write in the amount, subtract the check amount from the previous balance.

3. Double check your addition and subtraction. Mathematical errors can cause problems when you are trying to manage your money.

Name _____ Date _____

Post-Secondary Commitment Sheet

What is your plan? Will you complete post-secondary training, or go right into the workforce? If you have completed post-secondary training, this should be noted below.

First stage _____

Second stage _____

Third stage _____

Fourth stage _____

Remember that plans change, so if you decide to change your plan, mark the change on your plan and date it.

Name _____ Date _____

Post-Secondary Completion

This certifies that _____ has completed his/her post-secondary training on the date of _____, which will open many doors of opportunity.

_____
Signature of teacher

_____
Date

Vocabulary

balance—the amount of money in a checking account

check—a piece of paper officially allowing a withdrawal from a checking account

check register—a place to document checks, withdrawals, and deposits from a checking account; keeps track of account balance

deductions—amounts subtracted

deposit—money put into a checking account

FICA—Federal Insurance Contributions Act; includes Social Security and Medicare

financial transactions—a deposit into or withdrawal from a checking account

fixed expense—a bill that does not change amount

gross pay—the amount of pay earned prior to any deductions being taken out

installment loan—money borrowed for a short term that is paid back on a regular basis

Medicare—tax that is deducted from a paycheck to pay for hospital, medical, and prescription drug coverage for those who qualify

net pay—another name for *take-home pay,* the amount of pay after deductions are taken out

payee—the person a check is written out to

post-secondary training—school or training after high school

Social Security—tax that is deducted from a paycheck to provide retirement, disability, and survivor benefits for those who qualify

take-home pay—another name for *net pay,* the amount of pay after deductions are taken out

time sheet—a place to document the number of hours worked; turned in to the employer to receive payment for hours worked

utilities services—utilities provided to the home such as electricity and phone

What's Next? Auction Description

The *What's Next?* Auction is an optional activity that can occur after each stage (which for most teachers is at the end of the quarter). The auction allows students to decide if they are going to spend or save their money. The items to be auctioned off can be anything that is appealing to students. Some examples are extra credit, a free assignment card, pizza, or soda. The total number of items can vary. Many students will be tempted to spend all or almost all of their money, which can lead to a discussion about the importance of saving money.

Prior to the auction, students should register by turning in their current check register. This amount should be written down. You should double-check that students do not bid more than they have. You should assign each student a number and tell them the number.

Since the dollar amounts are higher amounts due to compressed time, the auction amounts often are higher as well. For example, the opening bid for a pizza may be $100, but it may eventually sell for $13,000. The experience of the auction, impulse buying, and the compulsion to spend more than you can afford can lead to stimulating classroom discussions.

Name _____ Date _____

What's Next? Auction Rules

Welcome to the *What's Next?* Auction. Today there are a limited number of items to be auctioned off. You will not know the number of items to be auctioned off or the actual items until they come up for auction. Here are the rules:

- The auctioneer has the final decision.

- A minimum bid will be established by the auctioneer. If no one accepts the opening bid, the item will be returned to the auctioneer.

- In order to bid on an item, you must have earned enough money according to your check register. If you bid on an item and you do not have enough money, you will be disqualified from the auction.

- In order to bid, you must be a registered bidder. You can only be a registered bidder if you have turned in a check register and had it approved by your teacher. If it is approved, you will be assigned a number.

- In order to bid, you must hold up your number clearly so the auctioneer can see it.

- The value of the item is determined only by the bidder. Some items will be sold for more or less than what you think they are worth.

- Inappropriate behavior will disqualify you from the auction.

- You can spend as much or as little of your money as you want. It is a personal decision. Any money you do not spend will be carried over to the next stage of the game.

- You can bid as many times as you want, as long as you have enough money to afford it.

Bidding Numbers

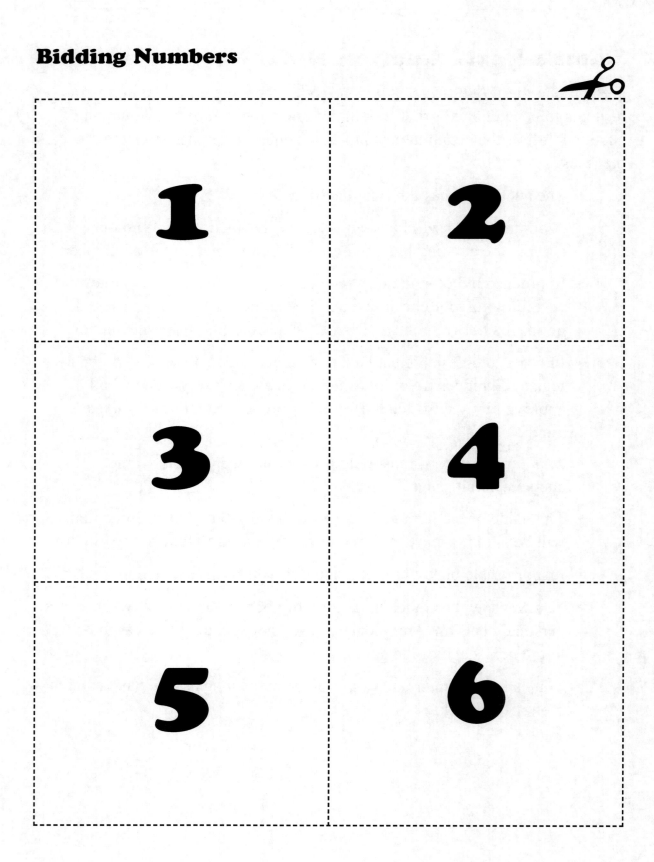

Bidding Numbers

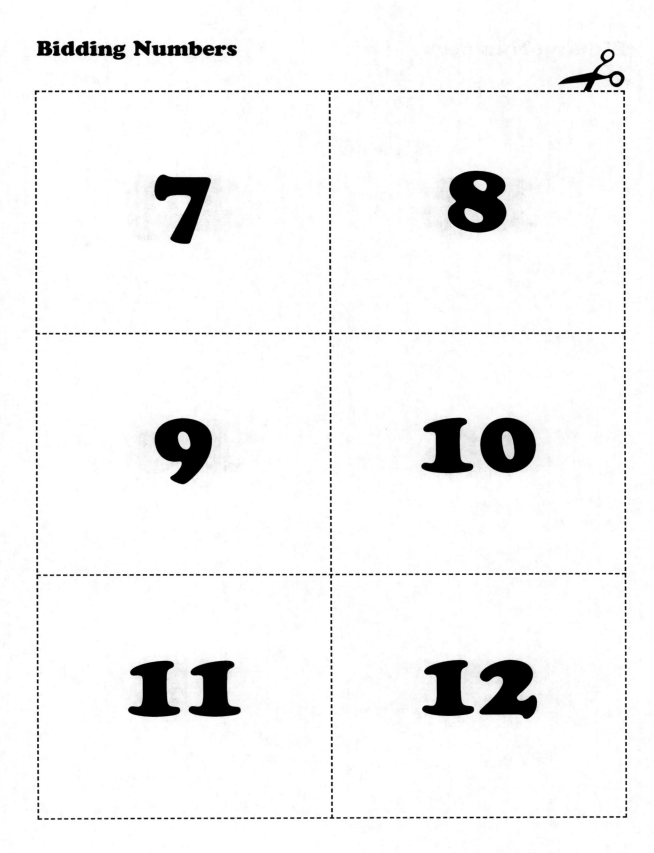

Bidding Numbers

13	**14**
15	**16**
17	**18**

Part 2

You Are Done with High School. Now What?

Implementation

This stage of the game requires the largest amount of teacher setup. After you have the first stage envelopes set up and organized, the amount of setup decreases with each stage.

To set up for this stage of the game, you will need the following materials:

- nine large office envelopes
- nine different colors of copy paper
- tape or glue
- use of a laminating machine
- a three-hole punch
- binders or folders for each of the students participating in the game (unless you require the students to provide their own)

Organizing the Simulation

It will help you and your students if you color code each of the large envelopes.

1. Copy the page titled "Time Sheet" on a sheet of colored paper. Laminate the sheet and attach it to the outside of one of the large office envelopes.

2. Using the same color paper, make copies of the time sheet to put inside the envelope. You will need one copy per student on a weekly basis.

3. Copy the page titled "Checks" on a sheet of colored paper. Laminate the sheet and attach it to the outside of one of the large office envelopes.

4. Using the same color paper, make copies of the check sheet to put inside the envelope. You will need approximately one sheet per student each week.

5. Copy the page titled "Deposit" on a sheet of colored paper. Laminate the sheet and attach it to the outside of one of the large office envelopes.

6. Using the same color paper, make copies of the deposit sheet to put inside the envelope. You will need one sheet per student every three weeks.

7. Copy the page titled "Check Register" on a sheet of colored paper. Laminate the sheet and attach it to the outside of one of the large office envelopes.

8. Using the same color paper, make copies of the check register sheet to put inside the envelope. You will need one sheet per student to begin with, and students will get a new copy as needed.

9. Copy the page titled "Rent" on a sheet of colored paper. Laminate the sheet and attach it to the outside of one of the large office envelopes.

   For the rent, you can decide to include rent payments for rural, urban, or both locations, you can allow your students to decide, or you can randomly choose where your students will live.

10. Using the same color paper, copy the sheets titled "Rent Payments." Laminate these sheets, and cut them apart. Then put them inside the envelope.

11. Copy the page titled "Cell Phone" on a sheet of colored paper. Laminate the sheet and attach it to the outside of one of the large office envelopes.

12. Using the same color paper, copy the cell phone payments. Laminate these sheets, and cut them apart. Then put them inside the envelope.

13. Copy the page titled "Car Payments" on a sheet of colored paper. Laminate the sheet and attach it to the outside of one of the large office envelopes.

14. Using the same color paper, copy the car payments. Laminate these sheets, and cut them apart. Then put them inside the envelope.

15. Copy the pages titled "Perks" and "Pitfalls" on sheets of colored paper. Laminate the sheet and attach it to the outside of one of the large office envelopes.

16. Using the same color paper, copy the perks and pitfalls. Laminate these sheets, and cut them apart. Then put them inside the envelope.

17. Copy the page titled "Loan Agreement" on a sheet of colored paper. Laminate one sheet and attach it to the outside of one of the large office envelopes.

18. Using the same color paper, copy the sheet with the loan agreement. Put several copies of the loan agreement inside the envelope.

19. Copy and laminate the page titled "Weekly Reminder Sheet," and post the sheet in the classroom. This can be used as a personal reminder for you, or as a reminder for students.

20. Copy and laminate the page titled "What You Need to Remember When Dealing with Bank Transactions," and post the sheet in the classroom.

21. Copy the "You Are Done with High School: Student Overview" sheet for each student in the class.

22. Make copies of the following pages for each student in the class: You Are Done with High School: Rules, the Fixed Expense sheet, the Completing Paperwork sheet, the Vocabulary sheet, What Will You Do After High School?, and the Post-Secondary Commitment sheet.

You can either provide or require each student to have a 1-inch binder or folder. The students will keep all of their *What's Next?* materials in the binder. It is helpful if the binder has pockets, so all the paperwork is kept together until you check each student's work.

To Begin the Game

1. Hand out the Student Overview to each student and explain the purpose of the game.

2. Hand out or require students to get binders or folders for the game.

3. Read and discuss the You Are Done with High School: Rules sheet.

4. Instruct students to put the rule sheet in the binder or folder for future reference.

5. Read and discuss the Completing Paperwork sheet.

6. Instruct students to put the Completing Paperwork sheet in the binder or folder for future reference.

7. Read the "What Will You Do After High School?" sheet, have students complete the Post-Secondary Commitment sheet, and include this in the binder or folder.

8. Discuss the Fixed Expense sheet. Students will only fill in their post-secondary educational choice, one auto payment and payee for an auto loan (which they can come up with on their own), their rent payment and landlord, and the provider for the cell phone bill.

9. Discuss the Vocabulary sheet. You may want to review the vocabulary as it becomes pertinent to the game, but each student should also keep a copy of the vocabulary sheet in his or her binder or folder.

10. Inform students where the materials for the game will be kept.

11. Instruct students to take a time sheet, complete the identification material, and keep this in the binder or folder.

At the Beginning or End of Each Class Period

1. Have students write in their attendance points and any assignment, project, volunteer, or miscellaneous points.

2. If there are any reminders, post them on the Weekly Reminder sheet.

3. On the day prior to the last day of the school week, have each student tally his or her take-home pay. At this point, taxes will not be taken out. To cut down on mistakes, have students check their partner's take-home pay.

4. Have students hand in their binder or folder at a predetermined place.

5. Review each student's calculations for take-home pay. If the student is correct, write out a paycheck for that amount. If the student is incorrect, mark the mistakes and deduct $100 for each error.

On the Last Day of the School Week

1. Hand back or have students pick up their pay binders or folders.

2. Post reminders on the page titled "What You Need to Remember When Dealing with Bank Transactions."

3. Have students select their first bill from the envelope (cell phone bill).

4. Have students select a pitfall or perk from the envelope.

5. Instruct students to pick up a sheet of deposit tickets, checks, and a check register, and put them in their binder or folder.

6. Have students deposit their paychecks and any perks they may have received.

7. Instruct students to write out the checks for their bills and any pitfalls they may have received.

8. Instruct students to enter the deposit and checks in their check register.

9. Encourage students to have their partner check their financial transactions and check register. To encourage accuracy of the financial transactions, correct financial transactions and an accurate check register could be rewarded a grade or miscellaneous points for the future week.

10. Have students begin a new time sheet and mark their attendance points. (In general, the time sheet will run from Friday to the following Thursday.)

11. Have students hand in their binder or folder. You can determine how they will be assessed.

Following Weeks

1. Continue with time sheets, deposits, checks, and perks and pitfalls.

2. During the second week, the bill is the car payment.

3. During the third week, the bill is rent.

4. After the third week, the cycle of bills starts over.

You Are Done with High School: Things to Consider

In this stage, the financial considerations include having a roommate, renting, purchasing a car, opening a checking account, buying a luxury item, and comparing credit cards. These tasks are to be done individually. You may decide to have students complete them any time it is conducive to your classroom schedule.

What's Next? Auction

At the end of this stage, which is generally a quarter of the school year, you can decide if you are going to hold a *What's Next?* Auction. If so, you will need to gather items to auction off. Items can be anything your students find appealing. Some examples include extra credit, a free assignment card, pizza, and soda. You could also solicit donations from area businesses such as free movie passes or food vouchers. Prior to the auction, you should copy the auction rules for everyone in the class, and copy, laminate, and cut the numbers apart for the auction. You will also need to collect everyone's check register, spot check them for accuracy, and record each student's balance for record keeping during the auction. This essentially registers the bidder. On the day of the auction, you should hand out bidding numbers, make everyone aware of the auction rules, and then conduct the auction. After the auction, you should have students who purchased items write out a check and adjust their check registers accordingly. You should also lead the group in a discussion about the value of certain items, impulse buying, and saving.

Name _____   Date _____

You Are Done with High School: Overview

Welcome to the start of your life in the game of *What's Next?*. During this
stage of "your life," you have just graduated from high school. As in real life,
there are going to be many decisions you have to make. One decision you
will be asked to make is about post-secondary training and/or work. At this
point, you will need to decide which route you will go. Many people at this
stage of life also move in with a roommate. Since most high school students
have only lived with their parents, moving out can be a very big change.
Most young people cannot afford to buy a house right away, so they will have
to rent an apartment. Furthermore, most young people need to have a
roommate to share the expenses, so they can afford to live on their own. You
will be asked to give some consideration to having a roommate—the pros and
cons, and the characteristics you desire in a roommate.

During this stage, you will be making "money" for going to class, but the
amount will depend on if you plan on attending post-secondary school or
training. You will also make "money" for the quality work you complete. The
You Are Done with High School rule sheet outlines the exact amounts you
can earn. The rule sheet also describes your responsibilities. The financial
responsibilities you will need to consider during this stage are housing
expenses, auto expenses, and your cell phone bill. The housing and auto
expense will be a fixed expense after you initially make your selection, so it
is important to note the amount and provider on the fixed expense sheet. The
provider for both of these is a personal decision, but you need to write down
the name on the fixed expense sheet, so you are consistent with your
payments. Your cell phone bill will be a variable expense because it will
depend on the amount of use. However, you need to be consistent on your
provider, so write down who you will be making your cell phone bill out to
on your fixed expense sheet. Throughout the game, you will also need to deal
with the financial perks and pitfalls you cannot always plan for.

Name _____   Date _____

In addition to the financial management component of the game, you will be asked to give careful consideration to other financial and personal decisions you will need to make when you are just starting out. You will need to give careful consideration to renting and having a roommate, purchasing a car, opening a checking account, buying a luxury item, and gathering information about credit cards. This exploration will hopefully open your eyes to what life will be like after graduation.

Name _____ Date _____

You Are Done with High School: Rules

Earning Money

- You are now getting "paid" to show up for class on time. You will earn $100 for daily attendance.

- If you are late for class, you will not earn the $100 for daily attendance. Showing up to work on time is very important and valued by employers.

- If you know you are going to be absent, communicate with your teacher prior to your absence. If you do this, you will not earn your daily attendance points, but you will not lose anything either.

- If you are too ill to come to school, call and leave a message for your teacher prior to the beginning of the school day. You must get in the habit of communicating with your employer if you will not be at work. It is also very important that you personally call in unless you are absolutely not able to call in yourself. If you do not call in on time, this will result in a loss of **$500.** Yes, that is steep, but not calling in when you are not able to work is a good way to lose a job.

- At the beginning of this stage, decide if you are going to pursue post-secondary training. If you do pursue post-secondary training (which you will declare on the Post-Secondary Commitment sheet), you will spend a considerable amount of time and energy on your studies. Therefore, during the post-secondary training stage, you will earn half as much for attendance points. You may quit post-secondary training at any time, but you will lose all that you have invested. You may only declare you are going to pursue post-secondary training at the start of each stage.

- You will earn money for completing quality work. An assignment in the "A" or "B" range is worth $500.

Name _____ Date _____

- You may be asked to complete projects, but generally a project requires more time and effort. Your teacher will differentiate between an assignment and a project. Therefore, a project in the "A" range is worth $1,000, and a project in the "B" range is worth $750.

- Exemplary classroom participation, behavior, and volunteer work may also earn you points. The point values to be earned are left to the discretion of your teacher.

- Poor behavior warranting disciplinary actions will result in a $2,000 fine. Inappropriate behavior will not be tolerated at a place of employment.

Organization

- Keep a current time sheet. Update your time sheet daily. Your time sheet documents positive and negative dollar values earned.

- Keep your current time sheet and current rule sheet in your folder or binder. In addition, keep all of your checks, deposit tickets, and check registers in your binder or folder. If any other material is included in your binder, you will have to pay a $50 penalty to your teacher.

- Document the assignment and project points earned on the day they are handed back.

- If you are absent on the day an assignment or project points are awarded, it is your responsibility to ask your teacher for the points you missed on the day you return. If you do not ask that day, it is up to your teacher whether or not points will be rewarded.

- Volunteer points and other miscellaneous points earned should only be written down on the day they are earned.

Name _____ Date _____

- Tally your time sheet one day prior to the last day of the week, so your teacher can use it to write out a check. If you are absent on this day, your teacher can decide if he or she is going to make you wait until the end of the next pay period to pay you, or write a check for you on the day the checks are issued. However, you will still be responsible for your bills.

- If you fail to put the binder or folder with your time sheet in the designated spot so your teacher can write out the paycheck, you will not get paid until the next week. However, you will still have to pay your bills.

- If you have mistakes on your time sheet, your teacher will subtract $100 for each mistake. If you are found to be dishonest, you will lose everything! Dishonesty is one reason why many people lose their jobs.

Dealing with Your Financial Transactions

- Since you are now an adult, every week you will be required to pay bills. For this stage, your bills include the following: housing, car payment, and cell phone bill. Pay your cell phone bill the first week, your car payment the second week, and your housing bill the third week; repeat the process. Your housing and car payments will be fixed expenses after you initially draw an amount from the provided envelope. Your cell phone bill will change as you draw a different amount from the provided envelope.

- Positive and negative events can happen that are beyond your control, so at the end of each week, you will have to draw a pitfall or a perk from the provided envelope. A pitfall is something you write out a check for and a perk is a deposit.

Name _____ Date _____

- On the last day of the week, you will write out a check for your bill and the pitfall (if you drew one). If a specific payee is not provided, you need to come up with an appropriate one. Use the phone book as a reference point. Always pay your rent, car, and cell phone payment to the same payee.

- On the last day of the week, write out a deposit ticket for your paycheck and any perk you may have received. Combine all of your deposits on one ticket.

- With the checks and deposit ticket you have written out, accurately and completely fill in the check register.

- Keeping accurate financial records, writing out checks, and filling in deposit tickets is very important. You can easily get yourself in financial trouble by making just a few mistakes.

- Your teacher will inform you how the checks, deposits, and check register will be graded.

Name _____ Date _____

What Will You Do After High School?

Finishing high school is a great accomplishment—typically 13 years of hard work resulting in a high school diploma. This time of your life will probably be very exciting, but also scary. The rest of your life is in front of you, and you have some very important questions to ask yourself and important decisions to make.

- What type of job or career do I want to do for the rest of my life? What if I am not sure?

- Do I want to go on to get more schooling? Do I need more schooling to get the type of job I want?

- What type of schooling am I going to pursue—technical college, trade or specialty school, public or private college?

- Which school will I go to? What are the admission requirements to get in?

- Can I get on-the-job training? An apprenticeship?

- Do I want to join the military?

- How will I afford the type of training I want to pursue?

These questions are just the tip of the iceberg as you begin to think about your future. It is important to reflect on these questions, and to answer them for yourself. It is your future, so *you* need to be the one answering the questions. Speaking with others, completing job shadowing, internships, and school-to-work activities, and visiting technical colleges and colleges can help you make your decisions. The decisions you make at this stage in your life can and will have a lasting impact on your life.

Therefore, for *What's Next?* you will need to make some decisions about your future. On the Post-Secondary Commitment sheet, you are asked to make the decision at the onset of the game, and then again at the

Name _____ Date _____

start of each stage if you are going to seek post-secondary training. As in real life, for the game you will need to make sacrifices if you pursue post-secondary training. Post-secondary training requires a big commitment, both financially and in terms of time. Therefore, while you are pursuing your post-secondary training, you will be earning only half the wages you typically would if you were not pursuing post-secondary training. After this stage, you will be rewarded for this commitment. You need to complete the entire stage of post-secondary training to reap the rewards for the remainder of the game. Furthermore, you may quit the post-secondary training at any time. If you quit, you will not be able to receive any of the future benefits. At the end of the first stage, the benefits will be explained to you in more detail. As in real life, you don't know what might happen in the future. You may decide to pursue your post-secondary training at the onset of any of the stages, but the post secondary commitment sheet must be completed and shown to your teacher for his or her approval.

Rent: Rural

$225 rent	$185 rent
$455 rent	$395 rent
$200 rent	$350 rent
$430 rent	$180 rent
$135 rent	$255 rent
$275 rent	$210 rent
$235 rent	$310 rent
$425 rent	$305 rent
$390 rent	$425 rent
$225 rent	$320 rent

Rent: Urban

$900 rent	$1,250 rent
$1,500 rent	$1,100 rent
$1,950 rent	$850 rent
$1,750 rent	$1,000 rent
$1,300 rent	$1,600 rent
$1,225 rent	$1,875 rent
$2,000 rent	$2,225 rent
$975 rent	$1,450 rent
$1,825 rent	$1,175 rent
$1,375 rent	$1,550 rent

Car Payments

$185.22 car payment	$336.89 car payment
$219.94 car payment	$325.12 car payment
$389.78 car payment	$216.85 car payment
$174.82 car payment	$278.99 car payment
$289.94 car payment	$154.67 car payment
$389.70 car payment	$323.35 car payment
$237.90 car payment	$94.29 car payment
$178.90 car payment	$333.78 car payment
$328.39 car payment	$249.71 car payment
$156.38 car payment	$338.38 car payment

Car Payments

$175.00 car payment	$211.50 car payment
$189.60 car payment	$327.90 car payment
$287.50 car payment	$436.35 car payment
$467.25 car payment	$145.20 car payment
$313.62 car payment	$245.88 car payment
$434.19 car payment	$299.35 car payment
$186.45 car payment	$234.93 car payment
$168.88 car payment	$249.37 car payment
$239.89 car payment	$183.90 car payment
$215.60 car payment	$438.38 car payment

Cell Phone Bills

$298.23 cell phone bill	$15.00 cell phone bill
$87.23 cell phone bill	$62.90 cell phone bill
$183.78 cell phone bill	$427.88 cell phone bill
$54.67 cell phone bill	$213.82 cell phone bill
$68.32 cell phone bill	$23.35 cell phone bill
$104.23 cell phone bill	$52.35 cell phone bill
$42.83 cell phone bill	$92.37 cell phone bill
$23.28 cell phone bill	$90.23 cell phone bill
$92.23 cell phone bill	$189.66 cell phone bill
$232.02 cell phone bill	$89.77 cell phone bill

Cell Phone Bills

$192.32 cell phone bill	$158.22 cell phone bill
$82.32 cell phone bill	$139.29 cell phone bill
$18.99 cell phone bill	$389.67 cell phone bill
$112.16 cell phone bill	$139.02 cell phone bill
$90.27 cell phone bill	$55.71 cell phone bill
$13.67 cell phone bill	$71.99 cell phone bill
$129.67 cell phone bill	$106.33 cell phone bill
$79.82 cell phone bill	$31.65 cell phone bill
$89.52 cell phone bill	$192.88 cell phone bill
$19.52 cell phone bill	$51.64 cell phone bill

Perks

$600.00 tax refund	$2,030.89 tax refund
$1,250.95 sold antique toys	$25.00 cash from car pool
$5.00 rebate on lightbulbs	$85.00 Christmas presents
$15.00 returned cans and bottles	$50.00 birthday gift
$20.00 returned an item to a store	$100.00 found a wallet and received reward
$15.00 found in washing machine	$20.00 found money in coat pocket
$30.00 sold old clothes	$40.00 mowed neighbor's lawn
$10.00 found money on the ground	$150.00 won on lottery ticket
$65.00 watched neighbor's dog	$200.00 helped cater a wedding
$300.00 sold things in Internet auction	$75.00 shoveled snow for neighbor

Perks

$100.00 Christmas present	$8,000.45 stock profit
$40.00 gifts from the holidays	$40.00 cash from car pool
$85.00 sold produce from garden	$45.00 sold old lawn mower
$1,000.00 won a lawsuit	$1,500.00 scholarship money (if attending school)
$304.00 tax refund	$5.00 on lottery tickets
$2.00 won on raffle	$20.00 helped friend with car repairs
$700.00 sold puppies	$35.00 babysitting
$200.00 bonus at work	$3.35 interest earned on savings account
$15.00 helped someone move	$25.00 returned bottles and cans
$875.00 bonus at work	$254.32 tax refund

Perks

$12,089.67 family inheritance	$50.00 raffle winnings
$364.23 garage sale profit	$50.00 gave plasma
$100.00 gave platelets	$985.88 sold items on the Internet
$265.00 yard sale profit	$100.00 won a contest
$20.00 babysitting	$50.00 friend paid you back
$200.00 worked overtime	$155.00 worked overtime
$75.00 worked overtime	$140.00 garage sale
$20.00 helped a friend	$250.00 sold baseball card collection
$550.00 tax refund	$3.00 rebate check
$10.00 rebate check	$7.00 rebate check

Pitfalls

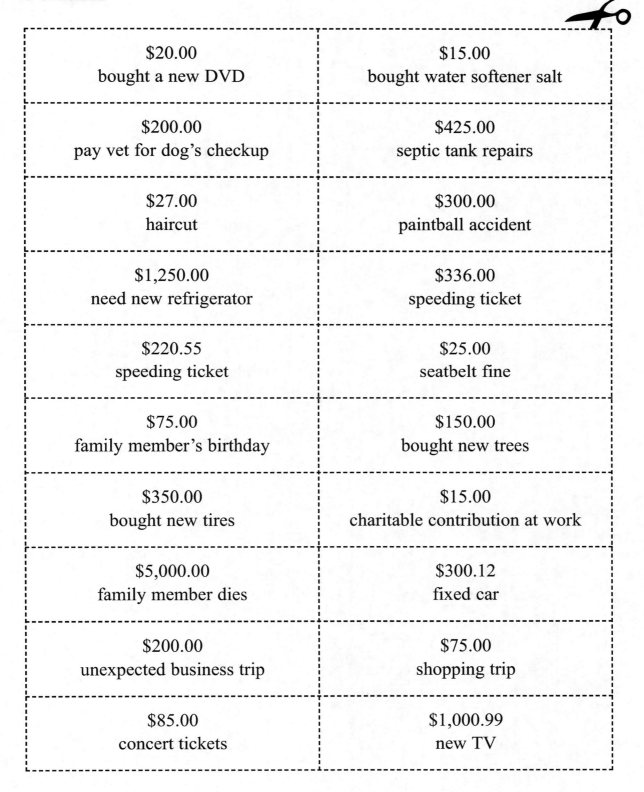

$20.00 bought a new DVD	$15.00 bought water softener salt
$200.00 pay vet for dog's checkup	$425.00 septic tank repairs
$27.00 haircut	$300.00 paintball accident
$1,250.00 need new refrigerator	$336.00 speeding ticket
$220.55 speeding ticket	$25.00 seatbelt fine
$75.00 family member's birthday	$150.00 bought new trees
$350.00 bought new tires	$15.00 charitable contribution at work
$5,000.00 family member dies	$300.12 fixed car
$200.00 unexpected business trip	$75.00 shopping trip
$85.00 concert tickets	$1,000.99 new TV

Pitfalls

$1,500.00 vet bills for your dog	$50.00 county fair
$50.00 father's birthday gift	$2,000.00 repairs from fire
$428.32 car repairs	$55.35 ordered new checks
$75.00 owed friend money	$267.32 unexpected credit card bill
$6,000.00 broke leg	$555.00 visit to the emergency room
$75.00 new shoes	$85.00 fertilized lawn
$5.00 library fine	$23.00 took friend out to eat
$20.00 baby shower gift	$19.56 new book
$6,700.00 pipes burst; pay for repairs	$25.00 parking permit
$97.33 carpets cleaned	$112.00 septic tank pumped

Pitfalls

$820.00 bought a new refrigerator	$135.00 bought a microwave
$560.00 bought new washing machine	$29.00 new waffle iron
$289.00 new vacuum	$510.00 new computer
$319.39 new camera	$60.00 treated yourself to a massage
$75.00 donation for research	$45.00 donation to charity
$25.50 haircut	$22.89 pictures developed
$320.00 new spring clothes	$55.00 highlighting
$890.00 new chair	$178.32 new printer
$133.03 shopping trip	$50.00 owed friend money
$35.00 fundraiser	$140.00 new glasses

Name _____ Date _____

Living with a Roommate
Good Idea or Bad Idea?

As an adult, it is common to have a roommate who is not a family member or spouse. However, many people often make the decision to have a roommate without giving it a lot of thought. It is very important to consider the pros and cons of having a roommate. It is also important to consider what characteristics and habits are important to you when agreeing to be a roommate. Complete the following chart.

Pros of Having a Roommate	Cons of Having a Roommate
Characteristics and Behavior You Want in a Roommate	**Characteristics and Behavior You Don't Want in a Roommate**

Name _____ Date _____

Renting

Answer the following questions.

1. If you are interested in renting a place to live, where could you learn about possible rental opportunities? List them below.

2. You can either rent an apartment or a house. List three things you need to consider when deciding which to rent.

3. List three advantages and three disadvantages of renting a home or an apartment vs. buying a home.

Name _____ Date _____

4. Before you start looking for an apartment or a house, you should make a list of things you would like to have or to be included in the apartment. Write your list below.

5. Besides the rent, what are some other expenses you will need to pay when you first move into an apartment?

6. Name ten things you will need to purchase when you live on your own. Find the cost of each, and be sure to name your source.

7. Find an apartment to rent. Write the description below.

Name _____ Date _____

8. Find a house to rent. Write the description below.

9. A common renter's rule states that you should not spend more than one week's income for rent. How much will you have to make per hour to be able to afford the rent for the apartment you listed in question 7?

10. How much will you have to make per hour to be able to afford the rent for the house you listed in question 8?

Name _____   Date _____

Purchasing a Car

Answer the following questions.

1. If you are going to purchase a new car, what questions should you ask? Write at least three below.

2. If you are going to purchase a used car, what questions should you ask? Write at least three questions below.

3. Name three places you could go to secure an auto loan.

4. What is the current interest rate for a new car loan for 48 months?

Name _____ Date _____

5. What is the current interest rate for a used car loan for 60 months?

6. Find a car you would like to purchase from a newspaper or on the Internet. Describe it below. Be sure to include the total cost, miles, miles per gallon, and warranty (if one is offered).

7. For the car you described in question 6, use an auto loan calculator (you can find one on the Internet) to determine a monthly payment for a 4-year loan with the current interest rate.

8. Name a place and phone number where you can get auto insurance.

Name _____ Date _____

9. Research if your state requires you to carry auto insurance. If it does, what type of insurance is required?

10. What is bodily-injury liability insurance? Define it.

11. What is collision insurance? Define it.

12. What are some factors that influence what you will pay for auto insurance? Name four factors.

Name _____ Date _____

Opening a Checking Account

Answer the following questions.

1. Name some items you should bring with you to open a checking account.

2. What is direct deposit?

3. What are two types of financial institutions where you can open an account?

4. You are ready to open an account. Name three factors you should consider when selecting a financial institution.

Name _____ Date _____

5. You need to choose the account that is right for you. Name three financial institutions you are planning to research.

6. Name three ways you can research the financial institution's accounts.

7. Using any of these three methods of research, complete the table below.

Name of Financial Institution	Type of Account	Perks of the Account	Drawbacks of the Account

Name _____ Date _____

Buying a Luxury Item

A **luxury item** is something you do not need but that you want.

Answer the following questions.

1. You just got a large inheritance. You have decided to spend all or part of the money on a luxury item. Name five items you would consider purchasing with this money.

2. For each of the items listed above, identify the specific cost and source of the cost.

3. Of the five items you listed, narrow your decision down to one. Why did you choose that item?

Name _____   **Date** _____

4.   Will the item you choose have any additional expenses that you will incur from its use or wear? List those expenses.

5.   How will this luxury item benefit you? List three benefits.

6.   What type of drawbacks could this luxury item have? List three drawbacks.

Name _____   Date _____

Comparing Credit Cards

Your task is to compare credit cards. An excellent web site to do this is www.creditcards.com. However, there are many sites on the Internet that allow you to comparison shop for credit cards.

1. Identify a credit card with a low interest rate.

2. For the card you chose above, identify the following:

   Intro APR _____

   Intro period _____

   Regular APR _____

   Annual fee _____

   Type of credit needed for the card _____

3. Identify another credit card with a low interest rate. For this card, identify the following:

   Credit card _____

   Intro APR _____

   Intro period _____

   Regular APR _____

   Annual fee _____

   Type of credit needed for the card _____

Name _____ Date _____

4. Identify a card that is described as a reward credit card. For this card, identify the following:

   What is the reward? _____

   Intro APR _____

   Intro period _____

   Regular APR _____

   Annual fee _____

   Type of credit needed for the card _____

5. Identify another reward credit card. For this card, identify the following:

   What is the reward? _____

   Intro APR _____

   Intro period _____

   Regular APR _____

   Annual fee _____

   Type of credit needed for the card _____

6. Identify a card that has a cash back program.

   How much cash back could you receive? _____

   Intro APR _____

   Intro period _____

   Regular APR _____

   Annual fee _____

   Type of credit needed for the card _____

   STOP

Part 3

Living on Your Own

Living on Your Own: Implementation

For this stage of the game, you will use many of the materials you have already set up. You will use the envelopes and following labeled materials: Time Sheets, Checks, Deposits, Check Register, Cell Phone, Perks, and Pitfalls, as well as the binder or folder for each student participating in the game.

For this stage, you need the following materials:

- two large office envelopes
- two different colors of copy paper
- tape or glue
- use of a laminating machine
- a three-hole punch

Organize the game by color coding the folders and materials.

1. Copy the page titled "Utilities" on a sheet of colored paper. Laminate the sheet and attach it to the outside of one of the envelopes.

2. Using the same color paper, copy the utility payments. Laminate these sheets, and cut them apart. Then put them inside the envelope.

3. Copy the page titled "Credit Cards" on a sheet of colored paper. Laminate the sheet and attach it to the outside of one of the envelopes.

4. Using the same color paper, copy the credit card payments. Laminate these sheets, and cut them apart. Then put them inside the envelope.

5. Copy the Living on Your Own: Overview and Living on Your Own: Rules sheets for each student in the class.

6. Copy additional time sheets, checks, deposit tickets, and check registers.

7. Copy the page titled "Taxes: They Never Go Away," the W-4 form, and the federal income tax charts for single individuals (weekly) for each student in the class.

To Begin the Game

1. Read and discuss "Living on Your Own: Overview" and "Living on Your Own: Rules."

2. Read, discuss, and complete the activities on the handout titled "Taxes: They Never Go Away!" (The tax forms and tables provided were the most current available at the time of publication. Use these forms and tables, or substitute the correct forms and tables for the current year. Current tax information can be found online at www.irs.gov, or at your local library or post office.)

3. Assist students in completing a W-4 for the game.

4. Remind students that the game will continue from the previous stage.

5. Review the Post-Secondary Education Commitment sheet, and have students update their sheet.

6. Discuss the fixed expense sheet. Have students update their post-secondary educational choice, and update their rent payment. The rent is now double. The car payment and payee, the landlord, and the cell phone provider will stay the same.

On the Day Prior to the Last Day of the School Week

1. Have students tally their take-home pay, and at this point, taxes will be taken out. (For the first few weeks, assistance will probably be needed.)

2. Have students hand in their binders or folders to a predetermined place.

3. Check each student's take-home pay calculations. If the student is correct, write out a paycheck for that amount. If the student is incorrect, mark the mistakes and deduct $100 for each error.

On the Last Day of the School Week

1. Hand back or have students pick up their binders or folders.

2. Post the reminder sheet, "What You Need to Remember When Dealing with Your Bank Transactions."

3. Remind students to double their rent from the first stage. That is their first bill.

4. Have students select a pitfall or perk from the envelope.

5. Instruct students to deposit their paycheck and any perk they may have received.

6. Have students write out checks for their bills and any pitfalls they may have received.

7. Instruct students to enter their deposit and checks in their check registers.

8. Encourage students to have a partner check their financial transactions and check register.

9. Have students begin a new time sheet and mark their attendance points. (In general, the time sheet will run from Friday to the following Thursday.)

10. Have students hand in their binder or folder. You will determine how they will be assessed.

Following Weeks

1. Continue with time sheets, deposits, checks, and perks and pitfalls.

2. During the second week, the bill is the car payment.

3. During the third week, the bill is the utility bill and the cell phone bill (if the student decides to keep it).

4. During the fourth week, the bill is the credit card bill.

5. After the fourth week, the cycle of bills starts over.

Living on Your Own: Things to Consider

In this stage, the financial considerations include a food allowance, furnishing a place to live, an entertainment allowance, and buying appliances. At this time, the exercises are to be done individually. You may decide to have students complete them any time it is conducive to your classroom schedule.

What's Next? Auction

At the end of this stage, which is generally a quarter of the school year, you can decide if you are going to hold a *What's Next?* Auction. If so, you will need to gather items to auction off. Items can be anything your students find appealing. Some examples include extra credit, a free assignment card, pizza, and soda. You could also solicit donations from area businesses such as free movie passes or food vouchers. Prior to the auction, you should copy the auction rules for everyone in the class, and copy, laminate, and cut the numbers apart for the auction. You will also need to collect everyone's check register, spot check them for accuracy, and record each student's balance for record keeping during the auction. This essentially registers the bidder. On the day of the auction, you should hand out bidding numbers, make everyone aware of the auction rules, and then conduct the auction. After the auction, you should have students who purchased items write out a check and adjust their check registers accordingly. You should also lead the group in a discussion about the value of certain items, impulse buying, and saving.

Name _____ Date _____

Living on Your Own: Overview

At the start of the next stage, you will have experienced life immediately out of high school. You will either be attending post-secondary school and working, or working exclusively. It is rewarding to get paid for showing up for work and doing quality work. However, as you have probably learned, the bills do not stop coming in and the pitfalls can be financially devastating.

During this stage, you will continue to get paid. The amount you are paid depends on whether or not you elected to pursue post-secondary training. Most individuals will quickly come to the realization that the sacrifice of post-secondary training is financially worth it in the long run. If you did not complete post-secondary training in the first stage, it's not too late to make the decision to continue your post-secondary training. As in real life, it is never too late to continue your education. But keep in mind that during the stage you decide to pursue your post-secondary training, you will have to make financial sacrifices, so it may be easier to pursue post-secondary training when you have fewer financial responsibilities.

Taxes

During this stage, there will be some changes. One change you must get used to very quickly is paying income tax. You were lucky to not have to pay taxes initially, as it allowed you to become familiar with how the game is played. When you start working, taxes will be taken out of your paycheck immediately. Furthermore, in this stage, you will complete a W-4 form, and you will deduct federal income tax, FICA, and Medicare from your gross income. Your teacher will determine if you will be deducting state income tax.

Monthly Bills

At this point in the game, you will not have a roommate. Therefore, the rent you paid during the first stage will still be paid to the same landlord, but now it will be double. You will also have to pay your car payment. You can decide

Name _____ Date _____

on an individual basis if the cell phone bill is something that is a necessity for you. If a cell phone is something you must have or you simply want to have, it is also a financial responsibility. You will be paying this bill along with the utility bill that you randomly select from the provided envelope. The final financial responsibility you will have is your credit card bill. However, as always, you will select from the financial perks and pitfalls envelope on a weekly basis.

Living Expenses

The financial questions you will explore at this stage deal with your food allowance, furnishing a place to live, purchasing appliances, and your entertainment allowance. You will probably find that as you bring in more money, your living expenses continue to rise. However, if you are financially savvy, you will be able to save money and accumulate a nest egg for yourself.

Name _____ Date _____

Living on Your Own: Rules

- You will continue to get "paid" to show up for class on time. You will earn $150 for daily attendance.

- If you are late for class, you will not earn $150 for daily attendance. Showing up for work on time is very important and is valued by employers.

- If you know you are going to be absent, communicate with your teacher prior to your absence. If you do this, you will not earn your daily attendance points, but you will not lose anything either.

- If you are too ill to come to school, call and leave a message for your teacher prior to the beginning of the school day. You must get in the habit of communicating with your employer if you will not be at work. It is also very important that you personally call in unless you are absolutely not able to call in yourself. If you do not call in on time, this will result in a loss of **$1,000.** Yes, that is steep, but not calling in when you are not able to work is a good way to lose a job.

- If you have completed post secondary schooling during the first stage, your hard work and diligence will pay off. You will now be paid double the daily attendance points.

- If you have not completed your post-secondary schooling at the beginning of this stage, you need to decide if you are going to pursue post-secondary training. If you do pursue post-secondary training (which you will have to declare on the post-secondary commitment sheet and on your fixed expense sheet), you will need to dedicate a considerable amount of time and energy to your studies. Therefore, during the stage of your post-secondary training, you will earn half as much for attendance points. You may quit post-secondary training at any time, but you will lose all that you have invested. You may only declare you are going to pursue post-secondary training at the start of each stage.

CONTINUE ➤

Name _____ Date _____

- You will earn money for completing quality work. An assignment in the "A" or "B" range is worth $600.

- You may be asked to complete projects, but generally a project requires more time and effort. (Your teacher will differentiate between an assignment and a project.) Therefore, a project in the "A" range is worth $1,250, and a project in the "B" range is worth $1,000.

- Exemplary classroom participation, behavior, and volunteer work may also earn you points. The point values to be earned are left to the discretion of your teacher.

- Poor behavior warranting disciplinary actions will result in a fine of $2,000.

Organization

- Keep a current time sheet, and update it daily. Your time sheet will document positive and negative dollar values earned. If you earn negative dollar values, you should have your teacher initial your time sheet.

- Keep your current time sheet and current rule sheet in your folder or binder. In addition, keep all of your checks, deposit tickets, and check registers in your folder or binder. If any other material is found in your folder or binder, you will pay a $50 penalty to your teacher.

- Document the assignment and project points earned on the day they are handed back.

- If you are absent on the day assignment or project points are awarded, it is your responsibility to ask your teacher for the points you missed on the day you return. If you do not ask that day, it is up to your teacher whether or not the points will be awarded.

Name _____ Date _____

- Volunteer points and other miscellaneous points earned should only be written down on the day earned.

- Tally your time sheet one day prior to the last day of the week so your teacher can use it to write out a check.

- If your teacher cannot easily find your time sheet or you fail to put it in your binder or folder, you will not be paid for that pay period. However, you are still responsible for your bills.

- If you have mistakes on your time sheet, your teacher will subtract $100 for each mistake. If you are found to be dishonest, you will lose everything!

Dealing with Your Financial Transactions

- Since you are an adult, you are required to pay bills every week. For this stage, your bills include the following: rent, car payment, utility bill, cell phone bill, and a credit card bill. Pay your rent the first week, your car payment the second week, your utility bill and cell phone bill the third week, and your credit card bill the fourth week. Then repeat the process.

- Choose if you want to continue having a cell phone. If you do keep your cell phone, pick a separate amount to be billed each time you pay your utility bill. The car payment will be the same fixed expense from the first stage. You will be living alone, so you will now have to pay double what you paid in rent. The cell phone bill and the utility bill will change as you draw a different amount from the provided envelope.

- Positive and negative events occur that are beyond your control. At the end of each week, draw a pitfall or a perk from the envelope. A pitfall is something you will write a check for, and a perk is a deposit.

CONTINUE

Name _____ Date _____

- On the last day of the week, you will write a check for your bill and the pitfall. If a specific payee is not provided, you need to come up with an appropriate one. Use the phone book as a point of reference. Always pay your rent and your car payment to the same payee.

- On the last day of the week, write a deposit ticket for your paycheck and any perk you may have received. Combine all of your deposits on one ticket.

- With the checks and deposit tickets you have written out, accurately and completely fill in the check register.

- Keeping accurate financial records, writing checks, and filling in deposit tickets are very important. You can easily get yourself in financial trouble by making just a few mistakes.

- Your teacher will inform you how the checks, deposits, and check register will be graded.

Taxes

Taxes are a reality when you work. You cannot get out of paying them. Starting at this stage, you will need to calculate and deduct from your weekly gross pay the tax contributions for FICA and Medicare using the percentages provided on the time sheet.

- Use the provided federal income tax forms, your marital status, and the withholding allowance to calculate your federal tax withholding to deduct from your weekly gross pay.

- Your teacher will give you instructions if you are to deduct your state income tax contributions.

Name _____ Date _____

Taxes: They Never Go Away!

When you get paid, your employer is legally obligated to deduct certain taxes from your paycheck. The amount you earn prior to these deductions is called **gross pay.** After taxes are deducted, the pay is called **net** or **take-home pay.** The tax deductions are listed on your pay stub. Your employer will deduct federal and state income tax (if applicable) from each of your checks. The federal and state income tax deducted is based on the amount of money you make, your marital status, and the withholding allowance on your W-4 form. The more money you earn, the higher your tax rate will be.

Another type of tax deducted from your pay is **Social Security tax.** You may not see the words Social Security on your pay stub, but the letters FICA may be used to represent this amount. **FICA** stands for *Federal Insurance Contributions Act.* The money contributed under FICA provides retirement, disability, and survivor benefits to citizens who qualify. FICA is a percentage of your earnings that you are required to contribute. Your employer will match the FICA amount you contribute. If you are self- employed, you are required to deduct Social Security at a much higher rate because there is no matching employer contribution. As of 2007, the Social Security tax rate was 6.2%, and the employee must pay up to the wage base of $97,500. The other part of FICA is the Medicare tax. As of 2007, the Medicare tax rate was 2.9% for the employee and the employer. The employer must withhold 1.45% of an employee's wages, and pay a matching amount for the Medicare tax. A person is eligible for Medicare if they have worked for at least 10 years in Medicare-covered employment, are at least 65 years old, and are a citizen or permanent resident of the United States. If you are under 65, you may be eligible if you are disabled. Medicare has several parts—hospital insurance, medical insurance, and prescription drug coverage.

Employers submit these contributions throughout the calendar year. In the month of January, your employer will give you a W-2 form that will inform you how much money you earned, and how much state and federal tax was

Name _____ Date _____

withheld for the previous year. With this form, you will file federal and state income taxes by April 15. If you have not contributed enough federal and state tax based on how much money you have earned and your marital status, you will owe the federal and state government additional tax money. You have to pay this money to the federal and state government by April 15 to avoid a penalty. If your employer has withheld too much money to pay your tax liability, you will receive the money back as a refund after you have correctly filed your taxes by April 15.

Your employer will calculate your weekly income tax withholdings for you, and they will automatically deduct the amount you owe prior to issuing you a check. However, for this game you will need to calculate your own tax liability using the federal income tax tables and charts provided, and the percentages on your weekly time sheet.

Name _____ Date _____

Taxes

Complete the exercises below so that you can practice calculating tax liabilities.

1. Federal income tax (Use the provided tables.)

    $894; Married; 1 withholding allowance _____

    $1,323; Single; 0 withholding allowance _____

    $456; Married; 2 withholding allowances _____

    $1,093; Single; 1 withholding allowance _____

2. Federal income tax (Use the provided tables.)

    $2,938; Married; 2 withholding allowances _____

    $3,001; Single; 1 withholding allowance _____

    $2,038; Married; 0 withholding allowance _____

    $1,920; Single; 0 withholding allowance _____

3. Determine your tax liability for Social Security using 6.2%.

    $983 _____

    $1,920 _____

    $429 _____

4. Determine your tax liability for Medicare using 1.45%.

    $892 _____

    $582 _____

    $1,892 _____

CONTINUE ➤

Tax Forms

Form W-4 (2007)

Purpose. Complete Form W-4 so that your employer can withhold the correct federal income tax from your pay. Because your tax situation may change, you may want to refigure your withholding each year.

Exemption from withholding. If you are exempt, complete **only** lines 1, 2, 3, 4, and 7 and sign the form to validate it. Your exemption for 2007 expires February 16, 2008. See Pub. 505, Tax Withholding and Estimated Tax.

Note. You cannot claim exemption from withholding if (a) your income exceeds $850 and includes more than $300 of unearned income (for example, interest and dividends) and (b) another person can claim you as a dependent on their tax return.

Basic instructions. If you are not exempt, complete the **Personal Allowances Worksheet** below. The worksheets on page 2 adjust your withholding allowances based on itemized deductions, certain credits, adjustments to income, or two-earner/multiple job situations. Complete all worksheets that apply. However, you may claim fewer (or zero) allowances.

Head of household. Generally, you may claim head of household filing status on your tax return only if you are unmarried and pay more than 50% of the costs of keeping up a home for yourself and your dependent(s) or other qualifying individuals.

Tax credits. You can take projected tax credits into account in figuring your allowable number of withholding allowances. Credits for child or dependent care expenses and the child tax credit may be claimed using the **Personal Allowances Worksheet** below. See Pub. 919, How Do I Adjust My Tax Withholding, for information on converting your other credits into withholding allowances.

Nonwage income. If you have a large amount of nonwage income, such as interest or dividends, consider making estimated tax payments using Form 1040-ES, Estimated Tax for Individuals. Otherwise, you may owe additional tax. If you have pension or annuity income, see Pub. 919 to find out if you should adjust your withholding on Form W-4 or W-4P.

Two earners/Multiple jobs. If you have a working spouse or more than one job, figure the total number of allowances you are entitled to claim on all jobs using worksheets from only one Form W-4. Your withholding usually will be most accurate when all allowances are claimed on the Form W-4 for the highest paying job and zero allowances are claimed on the others.

Nonresident alien. If you are a nonresident alien, see the Instructions for Form 8233 before completing this Form W-4.

Check your withholding. After your Form W-4 takes effect, use Pub. 919 to see how the dollar amount you are having withheld compares to your projected total tax for 2007. See Pub. 919, especially if your earnings exceed $130,000 (Single) or $180,000 (Married).

Personal Allowances Worksheet (Keep for your records.)

A   Enter "1" for **yourself** if no one else can claim you as a dependent . . . . **A** _____

B   Enter "1" if:
- You are single and have only one job; or
- You are married, have only one job, and your spouse does not work; or
- Your wages from a second job or your spouse's wages (or the total of both) are $1,000 or less.

B _____

C   Enter "1" for your **spouse**. But, you may choose to enter "-0-" if you are married and have either a working spouse or more than one job. (Entering "-0-" may help you avoid having too little tax withheld.) . . . . **C** _____

D   Enter number of **dependents** (other than your spouse or yourself) you will claim on your tax return . . . **D** _____

E   Enter "1" if you will file as **head of household** on your tax return (see conditions under **Head of household** above) . **E** _____

F   Enter "1" if you have at least $1,500 of **child or dependent care expenses** for which you plan to claim a credit . . **F** _____
(**Note.** Do **not** include child support payments. See Pub. 503, Child and Dependent Care Expenses, for details.)

G   **Child Tax Credit** (including additional child tax credit). See Pub 972, Child Tax Credit, for more information.
- If your total income will be less than $57,000 ($85,000 if married), enter "2" for each eligible child.
- If your total income will be between $57,000 and $84,000 ($85,000 and $119,000 if married), enter "1" for each eligible child plus "1" **additional** if you have 4 or more eligible children.

G _____

H   Add lines A through G and enter total here. (**Note.** This may be different from the number of exemptions you claim on your tax return.) ▶ **H** _____

For accuracy, complete all worksheets that apply.
- If you plan to **itemize or claim adjustments to income** and want to reduce your withholding, see the **Deductions and Adjustments Worksheet** on page 2.
- If you have **more than one job** or are **married and you and your spouse both work** and the combined earnings from all jobs exceed $40,000 ($25,000 if married) see the **Two-Earners/Multiple Jobs Worksheet** on page 2 to avoid having too little tax withheld.
- If **neither** of the above situations applies, **stop here** and enter the number from line H on line 5 of Form W-4 below.

- - - - - - - - - - - - - - - - **Cut here and give Form W-4 to your employer. Keep the top part for your records.** - - - - - - - - - - - - - - - -

Form **W-4**
Department of the Treasury
Internal Revenue Service

Employee's Withholding Allowance Certificate

▶ **Whether you are entitled to claim a certain number of allowances or exemption from withholding is subject to review by the IRS. Your employer may be required to send a copy of this form to the IRS.**

OMB No. 1545-0074

2007

1 Type or print your first name and middle initial.	Last name		2 Your social security number

Home address (number and street or rural route)	3 ☐ Single ☐ Married ☐ Married, but withhold at higher Single rate. **Note.** If married, but legally separated, or spouse is a nonresident alien, check the "Single" box.
City or town, state, and ZIP code	4 **If your last name differs from that shown on your social security card, check here. You must call 1-800-772-1213 for a replacement card.** ▶ ☐

5   Total number of allowances you are claiming (from line **H** above **or** from the applicable worksheet on page 2) — **5** _____

6   Additional amount, if any, you want withheld from each paycheck . . . . **6** $ _____

7   I claim exemption from withholding for 2007, and I certify that I meet **both** of the following conditions for exemption.
- Last year I had a right to a refund of **all** federal income tax withheld because I had **no** tax liability **and**
- This year I expect a refund of **all** federal income tax withheld because I expect to have **no** tax liability.

If you meet both conditions, write "Exempt" here . . . . ▶ **7** _____

Under penalties of perjury, I declare that I have examined this certificate and to the best of my knowledge and belief, it is true, correct, and complete.

Employee's signature
(Form is not valid unless you sign it.) ▶ _____   Date ▶ _____

8 Employer's name and address (Employer: Complete lines 8 and 10 only if sending to the IRS.)	9 Office code (optional)	10 Employer identification number (EIN)

For Privacy Act and Paperwork Reduction Act Notice, see page 2.   Cat. No. 10220Q   Form **W-4** (2007)

Deductions and Adjustments Worksheet

Note. Use this worksheet *only* if you plan to itemize deductions, claim certain credits, or claim adjustments to income on your 2007 tax return.

1. Enter an estimate of your 2007 itemized deductions. These include qualifying home mortgage interest, charitable contributions, state and local taxes, medical expenses in excess of 7.5% of your income, and miscellaneous deductions. (For 2007, you may have to reduce your itemized deductions if your income is over $156,400 ($78,200 if married filing separately). See *Worksheet 2* in Pub. 919 for details.) . .   **1** $ _____

2. Enter: { $10,700 if married filing jointly or qualifying widow(er)
$ 7,850 if head of household
$ 5,350 if single or married filing separately } . . . .   **2** $ _____

3. **Subtract** line 2 from line 1. If zero or less, enter "-0-" . . . .   **3** $ _____

4. Enter an estimate of your 2007 adjustments to income, including alimony, deductible IRA contributions, and student loan interest   **4** $ _____

5. **Add** lines 3 and 4 and enter the total. (Include any amount for credits from *Worksheet 8* in Pub. 919)   **5** $ _____

6. Enter an estimate of your 2007 nonwage income (such as dividends or interest) . . . .   **6** $ _____

7. **Subtract** line 6 from line 5. If zero or less, enter "-0-" . . . .   **7** $ _____

8. **Divide** the amount on line 7 by $3,400 and enter the result here. Drop any fraction . . . . .   **8** _____

9. Enter the number from the **Personal Allowances Worksheet,** line H, page 1 . . . .   **9** _____

10. **Add** lines 8 and 9 and enter the total here. If you plan to use the **Two-Earners/Multiple Jobs Worksheet,** also enter this total on line 1 below. Otherwise, **stop here** and enter this total on Form W-4, line 5, page 1   **10** _____

Two-Earners/Multiple Jobs Worksheet (See *Two earners/multiple jobs* on page 1.)

Note. Use this worksheet *only* if the instructions under line H on page 1 direct you here.

1. Enter the number from line H, page 1 (or from line 10 above if you used the **Deductions and Adjustments Worksheet)**   **1** _____

2. Find the number in **Table 1** below that applies to the **LOWEST** paying job and enter it here. **However,** if you are married filing jointly and wages from the highest paying job are $50,000 or less, do not enter more than "3." . . . .   **2** _____

3. If line 1 is **more than or equal to** line 2, subtract line 2 from line 1. Enter the result here (if zero, enter "-0-") and on Form W-4, line 5, page 1. **Do not** use the rest of this worksheet . . . .   **3** _____

Note. If line 1 is *less than* line 2, enter "-0-" on Form W-4, line 5, page 1. Complete lines 4–9 below to calculate the additional withholding amount necessary to avoid a year-end tax bill.

4. Enter the number from line 2 of this worksheet . . . .   **4** _____

5. Enter the number from line 1 of this worksheet . . . .   **5** _____

6. **Subtract** line 5 from line 4 . . . .   **6** _____

7. Find the amount in **Table 2** below that applies to the **HIGHEST** paying job and enter it here . . . .   **7** $ _____

8. **Multiply** line 7 by line 6 and enter the result here. This is the additional annual withholding needed . .   **8** $ _____

9. Divide line 8 by the number of pay periods remaining in 2007. For example, divide by 26 if you are paid every two weeks and you complete this form in December 2006. Enter the result here and on Form W-4, line 6, page 1. This is the additional amount to be withheld from each paycheck . . . .   **9** $ _____

Table 1				Table 2			
Married Filing Jointly		**All Others**		**Married Filing Jointly**		**All Others**	
If wages from **LOWEST** paying job are—	Enter on line 2 above	If wages from **LOWEST** paying job are—	Enter on line 2 above	If wages from **HIGHEST** paying job are—	Enter on line 7 above	If wages from **HIGHEST** paying job are—	Enter on line 7 above
$0 - $4,500	0	$0 - $6,000	0	$0 - $65,000	$510	$0 - $35,000	$510
4,501 - 9,000	1	6,001 - 12,000	1	65,001 - 120,000	850	35,001 - 80,000	850
9,001 - 18,000	2	12,001 - 19,000	2	120,001 - 170,000	950	80,001 - 150,000	950
18,001 - 22,000	3	19,001 - 26,000	3	170,001 - 300,000	1,120	150,001 - 340,000	1,120
22,001 - 26,000	4	26,001 - 35,000	4	300,001 and over	1,190	340,001 and over	1,190
26,001 - 32,000	5	35,001 - 50,000	5				
32,001 - 38,000	6	50,001 - 65,000	6				
38,001 - 46,000	7	65,001 - 80,000	7				
46,001 - 55,000	8	80,001 - 90,000	8				
55,001 - 60,000	9	90,001 - 120,000	9				
60,001 - 65,000	10	120,001 and over	10				
65,001 - 75,000	11						
75,001 - 95,000	12						
95,001 - 105,000	13						
105,001 - 120,000	14						
120,001 and over	15						

Tables for Percentage Method of Withholding

(For Wages Paid in 2008)

TABLE 5—QUARTERLY Payroll Period

(a) SINGLE person (including head of household)—

If the amount of wages (after subtracting withholding allowances) is:

The amount of income tax to withhold is:

Not over $663 . . . . $0

Over—	But not over—		of excess over—
$663	—$2,575	. . . 10%	—$663
$2,575	—$8,490	. . . $191.20 plus 15%	—$2,575
$8,490	—$19,931	. . . $1,078.45 plus 25%	—$8,490
$19,931	—$41,625	. . . $3,938.70 plus 28%	—$19,931
$41,625	—$89,913	. . . $10,013.02 plus 33%	—$41,625
$89,913	. . . .	$25,948.06 plus 35%	—$89,913

(b) MARRIED person—

If the amount of wages (after subtracting withholding allowances) is:

The amount of income tax to withhold is:

Not over $2,000 . . . . $0

Over—	But not over—		of excess over—
$2,000	—$5,888	. . . 10%	—$2,000
$5,888	—$18,038	. . . $388.80 plus 15%	—$5,888
$18,038	—$34,463	. . . $2,211.30 plus 25%	—$18,038
$34,463	—$51,925	. . . $6,317.55 plus 28%	—$34,463
$51,925	—$91,275	. . . $11,206.91 plus 33%	—$51,925
$91,275	. . . .	$24,192.41 plus 35%	—$91,275

TABLE 6—SEMIANNUAL Payroll Period

(a) SINGLE person (including head of household)—

If the amount of wages (after subtracting withholding allowances) is:

The amount of income tax to withhold is:

Not over $1,325 . . . . $0

Over—	But not over—		of excess over—
$1,325	—$5,150	. . . 10%	—$1,325
$5,150	—$16,980	. . . $382.50 plus 15%	—$5,150
$16,980	—$39,863	. . . $2,157.00 plus 25%	—$16,980
$39,863	—$83,250	. . . $7,877.75 plus 28%	—$39,863
$83,250	—$179,825	. . . $20,026.11 plus 33%	—$83,250
$179,825	. . . .	$51,895.86 plus 35%	—$179,825

(b) MARRIED person—

If the amount of wages (after subtracting withholding allowances) is:

The amount of income tax to withhold is:

Not over $4,000 . . . . $0

Over—	But not over—		of excess over—
$4,000	—$11,775	. . . 10%	—$4,000
$11,775	—$36,075	. . . $777.50 plus 15%	—$11,775
$36,075	—$68,925	. . . $4,422.50 plus 25%	—$36,075
$68,925	—$103,850	. . . $12,635.00 plus 28%	—$68,925
$103,850	—$182,550	. . . $22,414.00 plus 33%	—$103,850
$182,550	. . . .	$48,385.00 plus 35%	—$182,550

TABLE 7—ANNUAL Payroll Period

(a) SINGLE person (including head of household)—

If the amount of wages (after subtracting withholding allowances) is:

The amount of income tax to withhold is:

Not over $2,650 . . . . $0

Over—	But not over—		of excess over—
$2,650	—$10,300	. . . 10%	—$2,650
$10,300	—$33,960	. . . $765.00 plus 15%	—$10,300
$33,960	—$79,725	. . . $4,314.00 plus 25%	—$33,960
$79,725	—$166,500	. . . $15,755.25 plus 28%	—$79,725
$166,500	—$359,650	. . . $40,052.25 plus 33%	—$166,500
$359,650	. . . .	$103,791.75 plus 35%	—$359,650

(b) MARRIED person—

If the amount of wages (after subtracting withholding allowances) is:

The amount of income tax to withhold is:

Not over $8,000 . . . . $0

Over—	But not over—		of excess over—
$8,000	—$23,550	. . . 10%	—$8,000
$23,550	—$72,150	. . . $1,555.00 plus 15%	—$23,550
$72,150	—$137,850	. . . $8,845.00 plus 25%	—$72,150
$137,850	—$207,700	. . . $25,270.00 plus 28%	—$137,850
$207,700	—$365,100	. . . $44,828.00 plus 33%	—$207,700
$365,100	. . . .	$96,770.00 plus 35%	—$365,100

TABLE 8—DAILY or MISCELLANEOUS Payroll Period

(a) SINGLE person (including head of household)—

If the amount of wages (after subtracting withholding allowances) divided by the number of days in the payroll period is:

The amount of income tax to withhold per day is:

Not over $10.20 . . . . $0

Over—	But not over—		of excess over—
$10.20	—$39.60	. . . 10%	—$10.20
$39.60	—$130.60	. . . $2.94 plus 15%	—$39.60
$130.60	—$306.60	. . . $16.59 plus 25%	—$130.60
$306.60	—$640.40	. . . $60.59 plus 28%	—$306.60
$640.40	—$1,383.30	. . . $154.05 plus 33%	—$640.40
$1,383.30	. . . .	$399.21 plus 35%	—$1,383.30

(b) MARRIED person—

If the amount of wages (after subtracting withholding allowances) divided by the number of days in the payroll period is:

The amount of income tax to withhold per day is:

Not over $30.80 . . . . $0

Over—	But not over—		of excess over—
$30.80	—$90.60	. . . 10%	—$30.80
$90.60	—$277.50	. . . $5.98 plus 15%	—$90.60
$277.50	—$530.20	. . . $34.02 plus 25%	—$277.50
$530.20	—$798.80	. . . $97.20 plus 28%	—$530.20
$798.80	—$1,404.20	. . . $172.41 plus 33%	—$798.80
$1,404.20	. . . .	$372.19 plus 35%	—$1,404.20

SINGLE Persons—WEEKLY Payroll Period

(For Wages Paid in 2008)

If the wages are—		And the number of withholding allowances claimed is—										
At least	But less than	0	1	2	3	4	5	6	7	8	9	10
		The amount of income tax to be withheld is—										
$0	$55	$0	$0	$0	$0	$0	$0	$0	$0	$0	$0	$0
55	60	1	0	0	0	0	0	0	0	0	0	0
60	65	1	0	0	0	0	0	0	0	0	0	0
65	70	2	0	0	0	0	0	0	0	0	0	0
70	75	2	0	0	0	0	0	0	0	0	0	0
75	80	3	0	0	0	0	0	0	0	0	0	0
80	85	3	0	0	0	0	0	0	0	0	0	0
85	90	4	0	0	0	0	0	0	0	0	0	0
90	95	4	0	0	0	0	0	0	0	0	0	0
95	100	5	0	0	0	0	0	0	0	0	0	0
100	105	5	0	0	0	0	0	0	0	0	0	0
105	110	6	0	0	0	0	0	0	0	0	0	0
110	115	6	0	0	0	0	0	0	0	0	0	0
115	120	7	0	0	0	0	0	0	0	0	0	0
120	125	7	0	0	0	0	0	0	0	0	0	0
125	130	8	1	0	0	0	0	0	0	0	0	0
130	135	8	1	0	0	0	0	0	0	0	0	0
135	140	9	2	0	0	0	0	0	0	0	0	0
140	145	9	2	0	0	0	0	0	0	0	0	0
145	150	10	3	0	0	0	0	0	0	0	0	0
150	155	10	3	0	0	0	0	0	0	0	0	0
155	160	11	4	0	0	0	0	0	0	0	0	0
160	165	11	4	0	0	0	0	0	0	0	0	0
165	170	12	5	0	0	0	0	0	0	0	0	0
170	175	12	5	0	0	0	0	0	0	0	0	0
175	180	13	6	0	0	0	0	0	0	0	0	0
180	185	13	6	0	0	0	0	0	0	0	0	0
185	190	14	7	0	0	0	0	0	0	0	0	0
190	195	14	7	1	0	0	0	0	0	0	0	0
195	200	15	8	1	0	0	0	0	0	0	0	0
200	210	16	9	2	0	0	0	0	0	0	0	0
210	220	17	10	3	0	0	0	0	0	0	0	0
220	230	19	11	4	0	0	0	0	0	0	0	0
230	240	20	12	5	0	0	0	0	0	0	0	0
240	250	22	13	6	0	0	0	0	0	0	0	0
250	260	23	14	7	0	0	0	0	0	0	0	0
260	270	25	15	8	1	0	0	0	0	0	0	0
270	280	26	16	9	2	0	0	0	0	0	0	0
280	290	28	18	10	3	0	0	0	0	0	0	0
290	300	29	19	11	4	0	0	0	0	0	0	0
300	310	31	21	12	5	0	0	0	0	0	0	0
310	320	32	22	13	6	0	0	0	0	0	0	0
320	330	34	24	14	7	0	0	0	0	0	0	0
330	340	35	25	15	8	1	0	0	0	0	0	0
340	350	37	27	17	9	2	0	0	0	0	0	0
350	360	38	28	18	10	3	0	0	0	0	0	0
360	370	40	30	20	11	4	0	0	0	0	0	0
370	380	41	31	21	12	5	0	0	0	0	0	0
380	390	43	33	23	13	6	0	0	0	0	0	0
390	400	44	34	24	14	7	1	0	0	0	0	0
400	410	46	36	26	15	8	2	0	0	0	0	0
410	420	47	37	27	17	9	3	0	0	0	0	0
420	430	49	39	29	18	10	4	0	0	0	0	0
430	440	50	40	30	20	11	5	0	0	0	0	0
440	450	52	42	32	21	12	6	0	0	0	0	0
450	460	53	43	33	23	13	7	0	0	0	0	0
460	470	55	45	35	24	14	8	1	0	0	0	0
470	480	56	46	36	26	16	9	2	0	0	0	0
480	490	58	48	38	27	17	10	3	0	0	0	0
490	500	59	49	39	29	19	11	4	0	0	0	0
500	510	61	51	41	30	20	12	5	0	0	0	0
510	520	62	52	42	32	22	13	6	0	0	0	0
520	530	64	54	44	33	23	14	7	0	0	0	0
530	540	65	55	45	35	25	15	8	1	0	0	0
540	550	67	57	47	36	26	16	9	2	0	0	0
550	560	68	58	48	38	28	18	10	3	0	0	0
560	570	70	60	50	39	29	19	11	4	0	0	0
570	580	71	61	51	41	31	21	12	5	0	0	0
580	590	73	63	53	42	32	22	13	6	0	0	0
590	600	74	64	54	44	34	24	14	7	1	0	0

SINGLE Persons—WEEKLY Payroll Period
(For Wages Paid in 2008)

If the wages are—		And the number of withholding allowances claimed is—										
At least	But less than	0	1	2	3	4	5	6	7	8	9	10
		The amount of income tax to be withheld is—										
$600	$610	$76	$66	$56	$45	$35	$25	$15	$8	$2	$0	$0
610	620	77	67	57	47	37	27	17	9	3	0	0
620	630	79	69	59	48	38	28	18	10	4	0	0
630	640	80	70	60	50	40	30	20	11	5	0	0
640	650	82	72	62	51	41	31	21	12	6	0	0
650	660	83	73	63	53	43	33	23	13	7	0	0
660	670	86	75	65	54	44	34	24	14	8	1	0
670	680	88	76	66	56	46	36	26	16	9	2	0
680	690	91	78	68	57	47	37	27	17	10	3	0
690	700	93	79	69	59	49	39	29	19	11	4	0
700	710	96	81	71	60	50	40	30	20	12	5	0
710	720	98	82	72	62	52	42	32	22	13	6	0
720	730	101	84	74	63	53	43	33	23	14	7	0
730	740	103	87	75	65	55	45	35	25	15	8	1
740	750	106	89	77	66	56	46	36	26	16	9	2
750	760	108	92	78	68	58	48	38	28	17	10	3
760	770	111	94	80	69	59	49	39	29	19	11	4
770	780	113	97	81	71	61	51	41	31	20	12	5
780	790	116	99	83	72	62	52	42	32	22	13	6
790	800	118	102	85	74	64	54	44	34	23	14	7
800	810	121	104	87	75	65	55	45	35	25	15	8
810	820	123	107	90	77	67	57	47	37	26	16	9
820	830	126	109	92	78	68	58	48	38	28	18	10
830	840	128	112	95	80	70	60	50	40	29	19	11
840	850	131	114	97	81	71	61	51	41	31	21	12
850	860	133	117	100	83	73	63	53	43	32	22	13
860	870	136	119	102	85	74	64	54	44	34	24	14
870	880	138	122	105	88	76	66	56	46	35	25	15
880	890	141	124	107	90	77	67	57	47	37	27	17
890	900	143	127	110	93	79	69	59	49	38	28	18
900	910	146	129	112	95	80	70	60	50	40	30	20
910	920	148	132	115	98	82	72	62	52	41	31	21
920	930	151	134	117	100	84	73	63	53	43	33	23
930	940	153	137	120	103	86	75	65	55	44	34	24
940	950	156	139	122	105	89	76	66	56	46	36	26
950	960	158	142	125	108	91	78	68	58	47	37	27
960	970	161	144	127	110	94	79	69	59	49	39	29
970	980	163	147	130	113	96	81	71	61	50	40	30
980	990	166	149	132	115	99	82	72	62	52	42	32
990	1,000	168	152	135	118	101	84	74	64	53	43	33
1,000	1,010	171	154	137	120	104	87	75	65	55	45	35
1,010	1,020	173	157	140	123	106	89	77	67	56	46	36
1,020	1,030	176	159	142	125	109	92	78	68	58	48	38
1,030	1,040	178	162	145	128	111	94	80	70	59	49	39
1,040	1,050	181	164	147	130	114	97	81	71	61	51	41
1,050	1,060	183	167	150	133	116	99	83	73	62	52	42
1,060	1,070	186	169	152	135	119	102	85	74	64	54	44
1,070	1,080	188	172	155	138	121	104	87	76	65	55	45
1,080	1,090	191	174	157	140	124	107	90	77	67	57	47
1,090	1,100	193	177	160	143	126	109	92	79	68	58	48
1,100	1,110	196	179	162	145	129	112	95	80	70	60	50
1,110	1,120	198	182	165	148	131	114	97	82	71	61	51
1,120	1,130	201	184	167	150	134	117	100	83	73	63	53
1,130	1,140	203	187	170	153	136	119	102	86	74	64	54
1,140	1,150	206	189	172	155	139	122	105	88	76	66	56
1,150	1,160	208	192	175	158	141	124	107	91	77	67	57
1,160	1,170	211	194	177	160	144	127	110	93	79	69	59
1,170	1,180	213	197	180	163	146	129	112	96	80	70	60
1,180	1,190	216	199	182	165	149	132	115	98	82	72	62
1,190	1,200	218	202	185	168	151	134	117	101	84	73	63
1,200	1,210	221	204	187	170	154	137	120	103	86	75	65
1,210	1,220	223	207	190	173	156	139	122	106	89	76	66
1,220	1,230	226	209	192	175	159	142	125	108	91	78	68
1,230	1,240	228	212	195	178	161	144	127	111	94	79	69
1,240	1,250	231	214	197	180	164	147	130	113	96	81	71

$1,250 and over   Use Table 1(a) for a **SINGLE person** on page 38. Also see the instructions on page 36.

MARRIED Persons—WEEKLY Payroll Period
(For Wages Paid in 2008)

If the wages are—		And the number of withholding allowances claimed is—										
At least	But less than	0	1	2	3	4	5	6	7	8	9	10
		The amount of income tax to be withheld is—										
$0	$125	$0	$0	$0	$0	$0	$0	$0	$0	$0	$0	$0
125	130	0	0	0	0	0	0	0	0	0	0	0
130	135	0	0	0	0	0	0	0	0	0	0	0
135	140	0	0	0	0	0	0	0	0	0	0	0
140	145	0	0	0	0	0	0	0	0	0	0	0
145	150	0	0	0	0	0	0	0	0	0	0	0
150	155	0	0	0	0	0	0	0	0	0	0	0
155	160	0	0	0	0	0	0	0	0	0	0	0
160	165	1	0	0	0	0	0	0	0	0	0	0
165	170	1	0	0	0	0	0	0	0	0	0	0
170	175	2	0	0	0	0	0	0	0	0	0	0
175	180	2	0	0	0	0	0	0	0	0	0	0
180	185	3	0	0	0	0	0	0	0	0	0	0
185	190	3	0	0	0	0	0	0	0	0	0	0
190	195	4	0	0	0	0	0	0	0	0	0	0
195	200	4	0	0	0	0	0	0	0	0	0	0
200	210	5	0	0	0	0	0	0	0	0	0	0
210	220	6	0	0	0	0	0	0	0	0	0	0
220	230	7	0	0	0	0	0	0	0	0	0	0
230	240	8	1	0	0	0	0	0	0	0	0	0
240	250	9	2	0	0	0	0	0	0	0	0	0
250	260	10	3	0	0	0	0	0	0	0	0	0
260	270	11	4	0	0	0	0	0	0	0	0	0
270	280	12	5	0	0	0	0	0	0	0	0	0
280	290	13	6	0	0	0	0	0	0	0	0	0
290	300	14	7	1	0	0	0	0	0	0	0	0
300	310	15	8	2	0	0	0	0	0	0	0	0
310	320	16	9	3	0	0	0	0	0	0	0	0
320	330	17	10	4	0	0	0	0	0	0	0	0
330	340	18	11	5	0	0	0	0	0	0	0	0
340	350	19	12	6	0	0	0	0	0	0	0	0
350	360	20	13	7	0	0	0	0	0	0	0	0
360	370	21	14	8	1	0	0	0	0	0	0	0
370	380	22	15	9	2	0	0	0	0	0	0	0
380	390	23	16	10	3	0	0	0	0	0	0	0
390	400	24	17	11	4	0	0	0	0	0	0	0
400	410	25	18	12	5	0	0	0	0	0	0	0
410	420	26	19	13	6	0	0	0	0	0	0	0
420	430	27	20	14	7	0	0	0	0	0	0	0
430	440	28	21	15	8	1	0	0	0	0	0	0
440	450	29	22	16	9	2	0	0	0	0	0	0
450	460	30	23	17	10	3	0	0	0	0	0	0
460	470	32	24	18	11	4	0	0	0	0	0	0
470	480	33	25	19	12	5	0	0	0	0	0	0
480	490	35	26	20	13	6	0	0	0	0	0	0
490	500	36	27	21	14	7	0	0	0	0	0	0
500	510	38	28	22	15	8	1	0	0	0	0	0
510	520	39	29	23	16	9	2	0	0	0	0	0
520	530	41	31	24	17	10	3	0	0	0	0	0
530	540	42	32	25	18	11	4	0	0	0	0	0
540	550	44	34	26	19	12	5	0	0	0	0	0
550	560	45	35	27	20	13	6	0	0	0	0	0
560	570	47	37	28	21	14	7	1	0	0	0	0
570	580	48	38	29	22	15	8	2	0	0	0	0
580	590	50	40	30	23	16	9	3	0	0	0	0
590	600	51	41	31	24	17	10	4	0	0	0	0
600	610	53	43	33	25	18	11	5	0	0	0	0
610	620	54	44	34	26	19	12	6	0	0	0	0
620	630	56	46	36	27	20	13	7	0	0	0	0
630	640	57	47	37	28	21	14	8	1	0	0	0
640	650	59	49	39	29	22	15	9	2	0	0	0
650	660	60	50	40	30	23	16	10	3	0	0	0
660	670	62	52	42	31	24	17	11	4	0	0	0
670	680	63	53	43	33	25	18	12	5	0	0	0
680	690	65	55	45	34	26	19	13	6	0	0	0
690	700	66	56	46	36	27	20	14	7	0	0	0
700	710	68	58	48	37	28	21	15	8	1	0	0
710	720	69	59	49	39	29	22	16	9	2	0	0
720	730	71	61	51	40	30	23	17	10	3	0	0
730	740	72	62	52	42	32	24	18	11	4	0	0

MARRIED Persons—WEEKLY Payroll Period
(For Wages Paid in 2008)

If the wages are—		And the number of withholding allowances claimed is—										
At least	But less than	0	1	2	3	4	5	6	7	8	9	10
		The amount of income tax to be withheld is—										
$740	$750	$74	$64	$54	$43	$33	$25	$19	$12	$5	$0	$0
750	760	75	65	55	45	35	26	20	13	6	0	0
760	770	77	67	57	46	36	27	21	14	7	1	0
770	780	78	68	58	48	38	28	22	15	8	2	0
780	790	80	70	60	49	39	29	23	16	9	3	0
790	800	81	71	61	51	41	31	24	17	10	4	0
800	810	83	73	63	52	42	32	25	18	11	5	0
810	820	84	74	64	54	44	34	26	19	12	6	0
820	830	86	76	66	55	45	35	27	20	13	7	0
830	840	87	77	67	57	47	37	28	21	14	8	1
840	850	89	79	69	58	48	38	29	22	15	9	2
850	860	90	80	70	60	50	40	30	23	16	10	3
860	870	92	82	72	61	51	41	31	24	17	11	4
870	880	93	83	73	63	53	43	33	25	18	12	5
880	890	95	85	75	64	54	44	34	26	19	13	6
890	900	96	86	76	66	56	46	36	27	20	14	7
900	910	98	88	78	67	57	47	37	28	21	15	8
910	920	99	89	79	69	59	49	39	29	22	16	9
920	930	101	91	81	70	60	50	40	30	23	17	10
930	940	102	92	82	72	62	52	42	32	24	18	11
940	950	104	94	84	73	63	53	43	33	25	19	12
950	960	105	95	85	75	65	55	45	35	26	20	13
960	970	107	97	87	76	66	56	46	36	27	21	14
970	980	108	98	88	78	68	58	48	38	28	22	15
980	990	110	100	90	79	69	59	49	39	29	23	16
990	1,000	111	101	91	81	71	61	51	41	30	24	17
1,000	1,010	113	103	93	82	72	62	52	42	32	25	18
1,010	1,020	114	104	94	84	74	64	54	44	33	26	19
1,020	1,030	116	106	96	85	75	65	55	45	35	27	20
1,030	1,040	117	107	97	87	77	67	57	47	36	28	21
1,040	1,050	119	109	99	88	78	68	58	48	38	29	22
1,050	1,060	120	110	100	90	80	70	60	50	39	30	23
1,060	1,070	122	112	102	91	81	71	61	51	41	31	24
1,070	1,080	123	113	103	93	83	73	63	53	42	32	25
1,080	1,090	125	115	105	94	84	74	64	54	44	34	26
1,090	1,100	126	116	106	96	86	76	66	56	45	35	27
1,100	1,110	128	118	108	97	87	77	67	57	47	37	28
1,110	1,120	129	119	109	99	89	79	69	59	48	38	29
1,120	1,130	131	121	111	100	90	80	70	60	50	40	30
1,130	1,140	132	122	112	102	92	82	72	62	51	41	31
1,140	1,150	134	124	114	103	93	83	73	63	53	43	33
1,150	1,160	135	125	115	105	95	85	75	65	54	44	34
1,160	1,170	137	127	117	106	96	86	76	66	56	46	36
1,170	1,180	138	128	118	108	98	88	78	68	57	47	37
1,180	1,190	140	130	120	109	99	89	79	69	59	49	39
1,190	1,200	141	131	121	111	101	91	81	71	60	50	40
1,200	1,210	143	133	123	112	102	92	82	72	62	52	42
1,210	1,220	144	134	124	114	104	94	84	74	63	53	43
1,220	1,230	146	136	126	115	105	95	85	75	65	55	45
1,230	1,240	147	137	127	117	107	97	87	77	66	56	46
1,240	1,250	149	139	129	118	108	98	88	78	68	58	48
1,250	1,260	150	140	130	120	110	100	90	80	69	59	49
1,260	1,270	152	142	132	121	111	101	91	81	71	61	51
1,270	1,280	153	143	133	123	113	103	93	83	72	62	52
1,280	1,290	155	145	135	124	114	104	94	84	74	64	54
1,290	1,300	156	146	136	126	116	106	96	86	75	65	55
1,300	1,310	158	148	138	127	117	107	97	87	77	67	57
1,310	1,320	159	149	139	129	119	109	99	89	78	68	58
1,320	1,330	161	151	141	130	120	110	100	90	80	70	60
1,330	1,340	162	152	142	132	122	112	102	92	81	71	61
1,340	1,350	164	154	144	133	123	113	103	93	83	73	63
1,350	1,360	165	155	145	135	125	115	105	95	84	74	64
1,360	1,370	167	157	147	136	126	116	106	96	86	76	66
1,370	1,380	168	158	148	138	128	118	108	98	87	77	67
1,380	1,390	170	160	150	139	129	119	109	99	89	79	69
1,390	1,400	172	161	151	141	131	121	111	101	90	80	70

$1,400 and over   Use Table 1(b) for a **MARRIED person** on page 38. Also see the instructions on page 36.

© 2008 Walch Education

Utility Bills

$35.65 cable bill	$203.32 natural gas bill
$137.83 natural gas bill	$280.48 water and sewer bill
$119.32 electric bill	$146.43 electric bill
$189.45 water and sewer bill	$125.43 Internet bill
$85.20 cable bill	$103.67 phone bill
$38.93 phone bill	$98.32 electric bill
$293.32 water and sewer bill	$25.33 Internet bill
$60.32 cable bill	$164.32 water and sewer bill
$76.33 electric bill	$49.93 electric bill
$78.32 phone bill	$70.90 cable bill

Utility Bills

$115.04 electric bill	$179.90 electric bill
$30.29 electric bill	$89.32 natural gas bill
$210.19 natural gas bill	$123.93 cable bill
$36.20 Internet bill	$203.38 electric bill
$148.32 phone and Internet	$183.21 phone, Internet, and cable
$132.32 phone, Internet, and cable	$112.40 cable bill
$45.23 electric bill	$42.55 Internet bill
$87.32 cable bill	$198.22 natural gas bill
$129.90 electric bill	$124.78 phone and Internet
$92.32 phone and Internet	$28.37 electric bill

Utility Bills

$456.23 phone, Internet, and cable bill	$90.39 electric bill
$32.60 phone bill	$45.67 cable bill
$78.92 electric bill	$103.23 Internet and phone
$129.92 electric bill	$293.32 water and sewer bill
$304.56 water and sewer bill	$89.78 cable bill
$182.32 phone, Internet, and cable bill	$104.22 electric bill
$342.78 natural gas bill	$92.44 phone bill
$190.32 water and sewer bill	$56.32 electric bill
$83.23 electric bill	$98.32 water and sewer bill
$49.08 cable bill	$142.87 phone, Internet, and cable bill

Utility Bills

$23.22 The Sporthouse	No credit card bill
$155.23 FlexCard	$309.93 Bullseye
$41.20 JT Gas	$146.29 Country USA
$155.23 Wally World	$310.98 Jim's Lumber Yard
$123.56 JR's Gas Station Plus	$123.45 Bazic Credit
$657.89 Flex Card	$235.76 Bullseye
$2,033.96 Country USA	$43.45 JT Gas
$156.32 The Dress Card	No credit card bill
$133.83 Stylin	$289.39 The Sporthouse
$68.02 JR's Gas Station Plus	$59.83 Mary's Clothing Store

Credit Card Bills

$3,002.74 Jim's Lumber Yard	No credit card bill
$193.22 JT Gas	$203.44 Bazic Credit
$2,038.22 Wally World	$329.22 Mary's Clothing Store
$5,692.38 The Sporthouse	$322.29 FlexCard
$203.30 Bullseye	$279.92 Stylin
$810.39 Old House Clothes	$28.92 JR's Gas Station Plus
$39.39 JT Gas	No credit card bill
$2,903.32 The Dress Card	$29.81 Country USA
$82.89 Old House Clothes	$73.43 The Anything Card
$90.38 Mary's Clothing Store	$32.29 Bazic Credit

Credit Card Bills

$67.28 Bazic Credit	No credit card bill
$109.32 The Dress Card	$1,072.37 Jim's Lumber Yard
$3,029.32 Country USA	$11.20 JT Gas
$42.48 Stylin	$498.22 Bullseye
$892.38 Wally World	$19.38 Flex Card
$232.35 The Sporthouse	$673.45 Old House Clothes
$893.33 The Anything Card	$234.93 Mary's Clothing Store
$256.38 JR's Gas Station Plus	No credit card bill
$83.73 JT Gas	$411.42 Wally World
$563.39 Bazic Card	$382.38 The Dress Card

Name _____ Date _____

Your Food Allowance

Purchasing food is generally the third largest expense a family has. As food expenses increase, it becomes even more important to find ways to save money while grocery shopping. Here are some common ways to save money while grocery shopping.

- Know how much you are spending on groceries. Avoid buying impulse items because they're on sale.

- Most grocery stores offer savings cards. You can save a lot of money just by getting a card most stores offer for free.

- Shop sales, and when something you use often is on sale, stock up.

- Shop at larger supermarkets because they can offer lower prices.

- Always use a list, and stick to your list.

- Plan some of your meals based around what is on sale.

- If the store is offering a special when you buy more than one, only buy what you need. You will generally get the special price anyway.

- Check your cupboards and refrigerator before you go shopping.

- Use in-store and manufacturer's coupons. Watch for stores that double or even triple coupon values.

- Always get a rain check for a sale item that has run out.

- Watch the cash register to check for scanning mistakes.

- Break yourself of "brand" habits. Generic or store brands are generally better buys.

- Don't be deceived by the product wrapper. Check the per unit cost. (You may need to take a calculator with you.)

- Don't do all of your shopping at the supermarket. Some items will be cheaper at discount stores, such as toiletries and cleaning supplies.

Name _____ Date _____

To help you understand how much money it takes to feed a family, create a grocery list for a week. After the grocery list is compiled, find approximate prices gathered from a visit to the grocery store, store flyers, or the Internet. Most people do not have an unlimited amount of money to spend, so you must keep the grocery list to a level at or below the one you select. Keep in mind that you will need to feed your entire family on what you purchase.

Use the space below to draft your grocery list. Use another sheet of paper to compile the information your gather.

Grocery Budget

$65 a week for a family of 4	$129 a week for a family of 4
$89 a week for a family of 4	$109 a week for a family of 5
$55 a week for a family of 3	$98 a week for a family of 3
$100 a week for a family of 4	$125 a week for a family of 4
$140 a week for a family of 5	$105 a week for a family of 4
$110 a week for a family of 5	$135 a week for a family of 6
$155 a week for a family of 5	$120 a week for a family of 4
$130 a week for a family of 4	$130 a week for a family of 5
$140 a week for a family of 5	$110 a week for a family of 3
$145 a week for a family of 5	$90 a week for a family of 5

Name _____ Date _____

Furnishing a Place to Live

When you live at home, you probably don't give much thought to the "things" in your parents' home. When you move out on your own, you will quickly realize that most apartments are pretty bare when you move in. This activity will require you to think about all of the "things" you will need to live on your own, and their respective costs. There are times when you are given things by family members when you move into your own place, but for this activity, you are on your own. You will need to furnish your new home without help from anyone. Since most people don't have an unlimited amount of money to furnish where they live, you will need to furnish your new home with the randomly selected dollar amount.

Compile a list of items, their cost, and the places you can purchase them, so you can live independently. You can find this type of information from ads in the newspaper or on the Internet. As you compile the list, give careful consideration to what you really need to survive on your own. Some things you want to have may not be a necessity, especially if you have a restrictive budget.

Use the space below to start your list. Use a separate sheet of paper to gather and compile prices and store information.

Furnishing a Home

$5,000 to furnish your home	$2,500 to furnish your home
$1,900 to furnish your home	$2,600 to furnish your home
$3,900 to furnish your home	$4,100 to furnish your home
$6,000 to furnish your home	$1,250 to furnish your home
$10,500 to furnish your home	$15,000 to furnish your home
$8,000 to furnish your home	$4,000 to furnish your home
$5,100 to furnish your home	$8,700 to furnish your home
$9,250 to furnish your home	$3,500 to furnish your home
$6,800 to furnish your home	$3,750 to furnish your home
$4,300 to furnish your home	$9,010 to furnish your home

Name _____ **Date** _____

Entertainment Allowance

Do you like to go out almost every night of the week, or do you prefer to spend a quiet evening at home? Do you have a hobby that is quite expensive or one that costs almost nothing? The answers to these questions will have a direct impact on the amount of money you spend for entertainment. By the way, **entertainment** is anything you do for enjoyment. Have you ever examined how much money you spend in a week on entertainment? If you have ever opened your wallet and wondered, "How did I spend all my extra cash?" it might be time for you to examine how you spend your money.

For the next week, keep track of what you spend your money on and how much you spend. On a separate sheet of paper, record what you spent. Take this sheet with you everywhere, and write down everything you spend. For the first few days, it would be good to share your list with a classmate, teacher, or parent because you may be forgetting to write things down, and they can help jog your memory. After the week is over, go through the list, highlight all of the expenses that can be considered entertainment, and ask yourself the questions that follow.

1. Am I surprised at the amount of money I spent? Why or why not?

2. Did I need to spend that money? Explain.

3. Did I want to spend that money? Why or why not? Explain.

Name _____ Date _____

Buying Appliances

Answer the following questions.

1. What appliances do you think you need if you buy a home? List six appliances.

2. What are three things to look for when buying appliances? List them.

3. Go shopping at a store, look at store flyers, or search the Internet to find the cost for each of the appliances you listed above. Include where you found the price after the name of each appliance.

4. Find two refrigerators from the same company with a price difference of at least $300. Why does one cost more than the other? Be specific.

Name _____ Date _____

5. Find two different stoves. Describe both below. Choose one to buy. Why did you choose one stove over the other?

6. From the sources you found for your appliance prices, look to see if financing is available. If so, what are the terms of the financing?

7. Choose three appliances. On average, how long will each appliance last? List your sources.

8. Select one appliance and attempt to find the exact same appliance but for a different price. Include where you found each appliance, and the prices you found for each.

Name _____ Date _____

Savings

Answer the following questions.

1. Name three reasons why you should make it a habit to save money.

2. Name two reasons why it is difficult for some people to save money.

3. In your own words, explain the difference between a need and a want.

CONTINUE

Name _____ Date _____

4. Name three activities a person could do to help him or herself become a money saver.

5. Give three examples of formal savings plans.

6. Who could assist you with saving?

Part 4

You Are Married

You Are Married: Implementation

For this stage of the game, you will be using many of the materials you have already set up. You will use the envelopes and materials labeled Time Sheets, Checks, Deposits, Check Register, Cell Phone, Car Payments, Utility Bills, Credit Card Bills, Perks, Pitfalls, and the binder or folder for each student participating in the game.

To set up the game for this stage, you will need the following materials:

- three large office envelopes
- three different colors of copy paper
- tape or glue
- use of a laminating machine
- a three-hole punch

Continue to organize the game by color coding the folders and materials.

1. Copy the page titled "Spouse's Wage" on a sheet of colored paper. Laminate the sheet and attach it to the outside of one of the envelopes.

2. Using the same color paper, copy the spouse's wages. Laminate these sheets, and cut them apart. Then put them inside the envelope.

3. Copy the page titled "Health Insurance Premium" on a sheet of colored paper. Laminate the sheet and attach it to the outside of one of the envelopes.

4. Using the same color paper, copy the health insurance premiums. Laminate these sheets, and cut them apart. Then put them inside the envelope.

5. Copy the page titled "House Payments" on a sheet of colored paper. Laminate the sheet and attach it to the outside of one of the envelopes.

6. Using the same color paper, copy the house payments. Laminate these sheets, and cut them apart. Then put them inside the envelope.

    For the house payment, you should decide whether to include house payments for rural, urban, or both locations, allow students to decide, or randomly choose where they will live.

7. Using the same color paper you used for the sheet titled "Car Payments," copy the car payments. Laminate these sheets, and cut them apart. Then put them inside the envelope.

8. Make copies of the following pages for each student in the class: Are Men and Women Really That Different?, Health Insurance: Do You Really Need It?, and the W-4 sheet.

To Begin the Game

1. Read and discuss the You Are Married: Overview and You Are Married: Rules sheets.

2. Read, discuss, and complete the activities for Health Insurance: Do You Really Need It?

3. Have students update their W-4 forms.

4. Remind students that the game will continue from the previous stage.

5. Review the Post-Secondary Education Commitment sheet and have students update the sheet.

6. Have students select a health insurance premium.

7. Have students select their spouse's income.

8. Discuss the fixed expense sheet. Each student will update his or her post-secondary educational choice, marital status, withholding allowance, two car payments, and payee for installment loans (which they can come up with on their own), house payment and payee for the mortgage, spouse's wages, and health insurance premium.

On the Day Prior to the Last Day of the School Week

1. Have students tally their take-home pay. The taxes and the health insurance premium deductions will be taken out.

2. Have students hand in their binder or folder to a predetermined place.

3. Check each student's take-home pay calculations. If the student is correct, write out a paycheck for that amount. If the student is incorrect, mark the mistakes, and deduct $100 for each error.

On the Last Day of the School Week

1. Hand back or have each student pick up his or her binder or folder.

2. Post the reminder sheet, "What You Need to Remember When Dealing with Your Bank Transactions."

3. Have students pay their house payment.

4. Have students select a pitfall or perk from the envelope.

5. Instruct students to deposit their paychecks, their spouse's wages, and any perks they may have received.

6. Instruct students to write out the checks for their bills and any pitfalls they may have received.

7. Instruct students to enter their deposit and checks in their check register.

8. Encourage students to have a partner check their financial transactions and check register.

9. Have students begin a new time sheet and mark their attendance points. (In general, the time sheet will run from Friday to the following Thursday.)

10. Have students hand in their binder or folder. You will determine how they will be assessed.

Following Weeks

1. Continue with time sheets, deposits, checks, and perks and pitfalls.

2. During the second week, the bill is two car payments. Students should select two new payments from the envelope.

3. During the third week, the bill is the utility bill and the cell phone bill (if they decided to keep the cell phone).

4. During the fourth week, the bill is a credit card bill.

5. After the fourth week, the cycle of bills starts over.

You Are Married: Things to Consider

The financial considerations in this stage include buying a house, planning a family vacation, having celebrations, and planning for a baby. At this time, activities are to be completed with a partner—preferably one of the opposite gender. You may decide to have students complete them any time it is conducive to your classroom schedule.

What's Next? Auction

You can decide at the end of the stage if you are going to hold the auction. Follow the same procedure described on page 37.

Name _____   Date _____

You Are Married: Overview

For the purpose of the game, congratulations! You got married! Getting married involves many financial changes. For example, you will need to consider if you are going to change your W-4 withholding allowance. You will also be using a different chart when looking up or calculating your federal income tax withholding. Make sure you are using the charts labeled "Married." Another deduction to consider is health insurance. The provided handout will explain the necessity of it, and you will select a weekly health insurance premium deduction from the envelope. You will then deduct this amount from your gross pay.

After you get married, your life will change in many ways, which you will explore during an activity titled "Are Men and Women Really That Different?" For the sake of the game, you will be moving out of your apartment and buying a house. You will select a house payment from the house payments envelope, and you will add that to the fixed expense sheet. Other bills you will need to be aware of are the cell phone bill (if you elected during the previous stage to have one), two utility bills, two car payments (because you and your spouse will both need a car), and a credit card bill. As in other stages, the bills will be paid on a rotating basis. Life's pitfalls and perks will continue to be something you need to deal with on a weekly basis.

Marriage is a partnership, so the financial areas to consider will require you to collaborate with another individual in the class. For the sake of the game, you are not married to any particular person in the class. The activities presented will require a collaboration of ideas on different areas with someone of the opposite gender. Your teacher will give you instructions on how to pair up. Everything may seem clear cut to you, but your spouse may hold very different viewpoints. You will be asked to give consideration to purchasing a house, planning a family vacation, having celebrations, and planning for a baby.

Name _____ Date _____

You Are Married: Rules

- You are now getting "paid" to show up for class on time. You will earn $200 for daily attendance.

- If you are late for class, you will not earn the $200 for daily attendance. Showing up to work on time is very important and valued by employers.

- If you know you are going to be absent, communicate with your teacher prior to your absence. If you do this, you will not earn your daily attendance points, but you will not lose anything either.

- If you are too ill to come to school, call and leave a message for your teacher prior to the beginning of the school day. You must get in the habit of communicating with your employer if you will not be at work. It is also very important that you personally call in unless you are absolutely not able to call in yourself. If you do not call in on time, this will result in a loss of **$1,000.** Yes, that is steep, but not calling in when you are not able to work is a good way to lose a job.

- If you have completed post-secondary schooling during the first two stages, your hard work and diligence will pay off. You will now be paid double the daily attendance points.

- If you have not completed your post-secondary schooling at the beginning of this stage, you need to decide if you are going to pursue post-secondary training. If you do pursue post-secondary training (which you will declare on the Post-Secondary Commitment Sheet), you will need to donate a considerable amount of time and energy to your studies. Therefore, during the stage of your post-secondary training, you will earn half as much for attendance points. You may quit post-secondary training at any time, but you will lose all that you have invested. You may only declare you are going to pursue post-secondary training at the start of each stage.

- You will earn money for completing quality work. An assignment in the "A" or "B" range is worth $750.

Name _____ Date _____

- You may be asked to complete projects, but generally a project requires more time and effort. Your teacher will differentiate between an assignment and a project. Therefore, a project in the "A" range is worth $1,500, and a project in the "B" range is worth $1,250.

- Exemplary classroom participation, behavior, and volunteer work may also earn you points. The point values to be earned are left to the discretion of your teacher.

- Poor behavior warranting disciplinary actions will result in a $2,000 fine. Inappropriate behavior will not be tolerated at a place of employment.

Organization

- Keep a current time sheet and update it daily. Your time sheet will document positive and negative dollar values earned. If you earn negative dollar values, you should have your teacher initial it on your time sheet.

- Keep your current time sheet and your current rule sheet in your folder or binder. In addition, keep all of your checks, deposit tickets, and check registers in your binder or folder. If any other material is found, you will pay a $50 penalty to your teacher.

- The assignment and project points you earn should be documented on the day they are handed back.

- If you are absent on the day assignment or project points are awarded, it is your responsibility to ask your teacher for the points you missed on the day you return. If you do not ask that day, it is up to your teacher whether or not the points will be awarded.

- Volunteer points and other miscellaneous points you earn should only be written down on the day they are earned.

- Tally your time sheet one day prior to the last day of the week so your teacher can use it to write out a check.

Name _____ Date _____

- If your teacher cannot easily find your time sheet, or you fail to put it in your binder or folder, you will not be paid for that pay period.

- If you have mistakes on your time sheet, you will lose $100 for each mistake. If you are found to be dishonest, you will lose everything!

Dealing with Your Financial Transactions

- Since you are an adult, you are required to pay bills every week. For this stage, your bills include the following: housing, two car payments, two utility bills, cell phone bill (if you chose to keep the cell phone), and a credit card bill. Pay your housing bill the first week, your two auto bills the second week, your utility bills and cell phone bill (if applicable) the third week, and your credit card bill the fourth week. Then repeat the process. Since you are married and possibly starting a family soon, select two new car payments. After you select new car payments, they will be a fixed expense for the remainder of the stage. You will also be moving into a new house, so you will select a new housing fixed expense. After you draw an amount from the envelope, this payment will remain the same for the remainder of the month. The utility bills and credit card bill will change as you draw a different amount from the provided envelope each time. The cell phone bill, if you decide it is a necessity, will continue to be drawn the week you pay your utility bill.

- Positive and negative events occur that are beyond your control. At the end of each week, draw a pitfall or a perk from the provided envelope. A pitfall is something you need to write out a check for, and a perk is a deposit. On the last day of the week, you will write a check for your bill and the pitfall. If a specific payee is not provided, you need to come up with an appropriate one. Use the phone book as a reference.

- On the last day of the week, you will write a deposit ticket for your paycheck, your spouse's paycheck, and any perk you may have received. Combine all of your deposits on one ticket.

- With the checks and deposit tickets you have written out, accurately and completely fill in the check register.

Name _____ Date _____

- Keeping accurate financial records, writing out checks, and filling in deposit tickets are very important. You can easily get yourself in financial trouble by making just a few mistakes.

- Your teacher will inform you how the checks, deposits, and check register will be graded.

Spouse's Income

Since you are now married, you and your spouse will both be contributing to the family's finances. You will randomly select your spouse's weekly income from the provided envelope.

Taxes

Taxes are a reality when you work. You cannot get out of paying them. You will need to continue to calculate and deduct from your weekly gross pay the tax contributions for FICA and Medicare, using the provided percentages on the time sheet.

- Use the provided federal income tax forms, your marital status (remember, you are married now), and the withholding allowance to calculate your federal income tax withholding to deduct from your weekly gross pay.

- Your teacher will give you instructions if you are to deduct state income tax contributions.

Health Insurance

Health insurance is extremely important. Health expenses are very expensive, and buying your own health insurance policy is also very expensive. However, it is not wise to live without health insurance. Therefore, most employers offer health insurance as a benefit, but most employees need to pay a portion of the premium. Select your health insurance premium contribution at the beginning of the stage, and you will deduct it from your weekly pay.

Name _____ Date _____

Health Insurance: Do You Really Need It?

People normally assume they will be in good health. Many people try to live a healthy lifestyle to decrease the chance of illness. However, there are illnesses and diseases that cannot be prevented, even when you try your best to lead a healthy lifestyle. Any type of ailment or accident can occur at any time, which may mean a simple trip to the doctor's office, or months of treatment or medical care. Treatment for the illness or accident is often necessary to avoid further complications. However, treatment can be very expensive, and if you do not have health insurance, you can easily accumulate a large amount of medical debt in a very short period of time. When people are ill, they often cannot go to work, so they will have medical debt incurring and no money coming in. Medical bills are a primary cause of bankruptcy!

One benefit offered by some employers is health insurance. Health insurance provides money for treating an illness. The cost of health insurance coverage has increased dramatically in recent years, and individuals often can't afford to pay for health insurance coverage on their own. The health insurance premium is the amount one must pay on a regular basis, generally monthly, to retain medical insurance. The premium amount is dependent on the amount of coverage one has, and is a reflection of their chances of developing a serious illness. If medical insurance is a benefit you have from your employer, the employer generally pays a portion or a percentage of the premium, and you pay the rest. Even when you pay a portion of the premium, your financial responsibility does not end there. Most insurance policies have a deductible, which is a certain dollar amount for an individual or family that must be paid before the health insurance company will pay anything. After paying the deductible, the individual is still responsible for a portion or percentage of the bill. The premium, deductible, and an individual's personal responsibility will vary according to the employer and the plan. It is very important to understand your insurance policy, so you do not end up with unexpected medical expenses.

Name _____ Date _____

To have a better understanding of the cost of medical expenses, do some research to find the average cost for the following procedures. You can obtain the information from people who have first-hand experience receiving medical attention for these procedures, or by using the internet.

Procedure	Estimated Expense	Source
a routine doctor's visit		
a strep throat test		
a pregnancy resulting in a routine delivery		
a pregnancy resulting in a C-section		
a trip to the emergency room		
a visit to an urgent care center		
a chest X-ray		
open heart surgery		

Health Insurance Premiums

$35.00 health insurance premium	$42.50 health insurance premium
$109.00 health insurance premium	$62.75 health insurance premium
$74.50 health insurance premium	$37.00 health insurance premium
$56.90 health insurance premium	$89.22 health insurance premium
$91.00 health insurance premium	$115.00 health insurance premium
$72.50 health insurance premium	$18.00 health insurance premium
$31.00 health insurance premium	$65.44 health insurance premium
$29.25 health insurance premium	$101.22 health insurance premium
$38.77 health insurance premium	$78.34 health insurance premium
$54.22 health insurance premium	$46.00 health insurance premium

Spouse's Weekly Wages

$322.90 spouse's weekly wage	$482.93 spouse's weekly wage
$554.83 spouse's weekly wage	$0 spouse's weekly wage
$378.67 spouse's weekly wage	$889.70 spouse's weekly wage
$982.32 spouse's weekly wage	$930.25 spouse's weekly wage
$764.20 spouse's weekly wage	$429.33 spouse's weekly wage
$1,293.83 spouse's weekly wage	$723.93 spouse's weekly wage
$1,289.31 spouse's weekly wage	$1,567.32 spouse's weekly wage
$1,067.89 spouse's weekly wage	$872.55 spouse's weekly wage
$1,617.44 spouse's weekly wage	$355.92 spouse's weekly wage
$622.19 spouse's weekly wage	$817.49 spouse's weekly wage

House Payments: Rural

$1255.90 house payment	$1,200.32 house payment
$983.32 house payment	$489.87 house payment
$778.83 house payment	$1,098.23 house payment
$1,398.12 house payment	$895.22 house payment
$789.25 house payment	$1,498.39 house payment
$1,389.24 house payment	$1,693.33 house payment
$983.92 house payment	$906.48 house payment
$1,089.20 house payment	$883.29 house payment
$938.29 house payment	$1,112.83 house payment
$897.25 house payment	$1,489.25 house payment

House Payments: Urban

$2,149.24 house payment	$1,874.28 house payment
$2,832.94 house payment	$1,584.83 house payment
$1,975.39 house payment	$2,764.83 house payment
$3,148.71 house payment	$1,764.55 house payment
$2,687.23 house payment	$3,001.91 house payment
$2,148.48 house payment	$2,234.19 house payment
$2,943.28 house payment	$2,387.33 house payment
$1,899.44 house payment	$2,540.39 house payment
$2,932.88 house payment	$1,779.11 house payment
$2,888.73 house payment	$3,238.88 house payment

Additional Car Payments

$375 car payment	$283.22 car payment
$390.39 car payment	$138.22 car payment
$277.65 car payment	$426.45 car payment
$437.17 car payment	$245.20 car payment
$412.27 car payment	$345.78 car payment
$404.29 car payment	$489.25 car payment
$326.45 car payment	$214.78 car payment
$198.28 car payment	$209.45 car payment
$189.78 car payment	$177.60 car payment
$315.42 car payment	$418.38 car payment

Additional Car Payments

$275.00 car payment	$483.22 car payment
$199.87 car payment	$128.72 car payment
$377.77 car payment	$296.65 car payment
$357.97 car payment	$185.31 car payment
$402.67 car payment	$235.68 car payment
$394.29 car payment	$422.25 car payment
$337.65 car payment	$298.78 car payment
$158.23 car payment	$212.32 car payment
$139.65 car payment	$217.89 car payment
$305.42 car payment	$411.20 car payment

Name _____ Date _____

Are Men and Women Really That Different?

The book *Men Are from Mars, Women Are from Venus,* written by John Gray, makes the claim that men and women are so different that they should be from two different planets. This exercise will require you to communicate with an individual of the opposite gender to decide if men and women really are that different. You and a person from the opposite gender will be asked to answer the questions in the categories listed below. Each of you should contribute your thoughts on the questions. Respond using different color inks to differentiate your opinions.

Money

1. You and your spouse just got a large tax return. How would you spend it—a big screen TV, a vacation for the family, pay off existing bills, or put it in a savings account? Explain.

2. Your family is considering spending money every month on a satellite dish that will allow you to access every channel available. The cost will be considerably more than what you are currently spending on cable. What are your thoughts?

Name _____ Date _____

3. Your spouse wants you to give up your hobby (such as bowling) because it costs too much. However, he or she continues to do something he or she enjoys once a month (for example, going shopping, playing golf, going out to dinner with friends, getting a massage), which costs more than your hobby. How would you handle this?

4. You get a letter from the bank saying you have bounced two checks. Your spouse reconciles the checkbook, but you wrote the checks without telling her or him. How do you resolve this problem so it doesn't happen again?

Name _____ Date _____

Communication

1. You and your spouse just had a disagreement. How do you react? Explain.

2. You are upset with your spouse because he or she forgot to call when staying late for work. What is your reaction? Explain.

3. You just had an awful day at work. Will you share your experience with your spouse? How do you want him or her to react? Explain.

4. Your spouse is dancing with his or her high school sweetheart. How does this make you feel and how would you react? Explain.

Name _____ Date _____

Time

1. You and your spouse both work outside the home. How will you split up the household chores? Explain.

2. How will you spend your time on Sundays? Will you be glued to the TV, watching sports, shopping, or doing other family activities? Explain.

3. You need to leave for a party in 5 minutes. Your spouse has not even started getting ready. How do you react? Will it bother you to be late? Explain.

4. Your spouse works out of your home. You have two kids at home who require his or her time as well. Your spouse does a lot of work at night after you are home from work. How do you make time for each other? Explain.

Name _____ Date _____

Sharing Space

1. Your spouse always leaves a mess in the bathroom after he or she is done? Does this bother you? How will you react? Explain.

2. You both leave for work at the same time, and you both like to sleep as late as possible. How will you decide who gets up first to get ready? Explain.

3. Your spouse's clothes take up most of the closet, leaving you little space for your clothes. How do you handle this? Explain.

4. When you just need to be alone, how will you explain this so you don't hurt your spouse's feelings?

Name _____   Date _____

Children

1. Your children are picky eaters. How do you handle the situation?

2. When your children misbehave, how do you think they should be disciplined? Explain.

3. Your elementary-age children are constantly fighting. How do you handle it?

4. Your children are involved in several after-school activities, which requires you to transport them to their activities almost every night of the week. How do you feel about this?

Name _____ Date _____

In-Laws

1. How often do you think you should visit your parents and your in-laws? Explain.

2. Your in-laws drop by your house without any notice. How do you feel about this? Explain.

3. Your mother-in-law is constantly criticizing you. How do you handle this?

4. Your parents and your in-laws are both having a celebration on the same day. Both want to see your young children, but the children haven't had a nap. How will you work this out?

Name _____   Date _____

Buying a House

When purchasing a house, there are many things to consider, including price, a down payment, monthly payments, the layout, the maintenance, property taxes, and much more.

1. To begin this exercise, brainstorm about your dream home. List what you really want in a home.

    Have your partner list what he or she really wants in a home.

    Compare your lists. How are they similar and different?

    Together, compromise and write a description for a home you would be interested in buying.

Name _____ Date _____

2. Use the Internet or classified ads to find three homes. One home should cost approximately $100,000, another home should cost approximately $250,000, and a third home you can choose based on your preferences. On a separate sheet of paper, write a description for each home. Each description should include a minimum cost for the home, dimensions, and an overall description of the home's features.

3. When purchasing a home, you need to pay a down payment. If the bank expects a 20% down payment, calculate the down payment for each of the homes you chose.

   $100,000 home _____

   $250,000 home _____

   Your choice home _____

4. For each of the homes above, use a loan calculator and the current home interest rate to determine the monthly mortgage payment for each of these homes, given a 30-year fixed interest loan. (Many loan calculators can be found online.) Don't forget to subtract the down payment amount from the loan amount before you calculate the monthly payment.

   $100,000 home _____

   $250,000 home _____

   Your choice home _____

Name _____   Date _____

5. With this information, select the home you think you can afford. Most families spend approximately 20 to 30% of their annual income on housing expenses. How much money will you have to make per year to be able to afford the monthly payments for a home of your choice?

6. Using information from the Internet or from other sources, estimate what the property taxes might be for this home in your area.

7. How much will you have to set aside on a monthly basis to pay for your property taxes?

Name _____ Date _____

Celebrations

Most people look forward to family celebrations, and many families have unique celebrations and traditions. Many people have certain traditions and beliefs on how things should be done. These beliefs are often deeply rooted, so when you are in a relationship, those traditions and beliefs may contradict one another, which can cause stress. Communication and compromise are often very important for having celebrations without too much stress.

1. With your partner, make a list of all the celebrations you have during a calendar year. You each should use a different color ink to make your list.

2. Compare your lists and select one celebration you have in common. Discuss and write down the key elements of how you both celebrate. You each should use a different colored ink.

3. Since everyone's celebrations are unique, there are probably some differences between your celebration and your partner's celebration. Write down at least one difference and how you would resolve it.

Name _____ Date _____

Having a Baby

A baby changes your life. A baby will change how you spend your time and your money. A baby is a gift that will bring much joy and happiness, but you must be mentally and financially prepared to care for a child. By answering the questions below, hopefully you will gain a better understanding of the financial and emotional challenges a baby presents when he or she enters this world. Some of the answers may be found in books or on the Internet, but others you can easily learn by asking anyone who has a child. Ask someone who has a baby and they will help you answer these questions, and probably tell you more than you wanted to know!

1. How many diapers does a newborn use in a day? How many packages of diapers will you have to buy a month, and how much will the diapers cost?

2. List seven things you will need for your baby.

Name _____ Date _____

3. How many times does a one-month-old infant wake up at night? How often does a one-year-old baby wake up at night?

4. Let's say you are going to use formula to feed your baby. Find the cost of a can of formula. How long does a can of formula last? How much will formula cost for one year?

5. It is recommended that you breastfeed your baby. Give three reasons why you should consider doing this.

6. How often do newborns eat?

Name _____ Date _____

7. How often you are supposed to take your baby to the doctor during the first year? Do some research, and write down all the ages (weeks, months) that you should take your baby to a doctor.

8. How much does a normal pregnancy cost, from the time you confirm your pregnancy with the doctor until you take the baby home after giving birth?

9. Jaundice is common in newborns. What is jaundice, and how is it treated?

10. What is SIDS, and what is the best way to prevent SIDS?

Name _____ Date _____

11. Your baby is sick. When should you take the baby to the doctor?

12. Most people take their babies to pediatricians. What is a pediatrician, and how will you go about choosing one?

Name _____   Date _____

Going on Vacation

Vacation! Whether it is in a sunny, warm climate, or in a cold, frosty one, vacation is something that most people look forward to. However, a vacation can be disastrous if forethought is not given to the details of planning one. This exercise will require you to give some careful consideration to vacation planning. You may need to use multiple sources for your research. Keep in mind that you will complete this activity with a partner. If you have different opinions, use a different color ink.

1. How will you decide where you will go on vacation? Explain.

2. How can you estimate what your vacation will cost?

3. What are some things you can do to save money while on vacation? List as many as you can think of below.

Name _____ Date _____

4. What are some things you can do to plan for and save in advance of your vacation? List some ideas.

5. Some families don't go on long vacations—they may go on local daytrips instead. Find out the cost of the following:

   • the cost to go to a Major League Baseball game (include four tickets, four sodas, and four hot dogs)

   • the cost to go to the zoo for a family of four (include parking)

   • the cost for a family of four to go to a large amusement park such as Disney World

6. You and your spouse want to go on a two-week vacation. On another sheet of paper, describe your vacation in detail. (Don't forget to include estimated prices for each vacation. This might take some research.) Where will you go? How will you get there? Where will you stay? Will you need to rent a car? What will you do while you are there? What will you do for meals?

Part 5

You Have a Family

You Have a Family: Implementation

For this stage of the game, you will be using many of the materials you have already set up. You will use the envelopes and materials labeled Time Sheets, Checks, Deposits, Check Register, Cell Phone, Car Payments, Utilities, Credit Card Bills, House Payments, Life's Pitfalls and Perks, and the binder or folder for each student participating in the game.

To set up the game for this stage, you will need the following materials:

- four large office envelopes
- four different colors of copy paper
- tape or glue
- use of a laminating machine
- a three-hole punch

You will want to continue to organize the game by color coding the folders and materials.

1. Copy the page titled "Number and Age of Children" on a sheet of colored paper. Laminate the sheet and attach it to the outside of one of the envelopes.

2. Using the same color paper, copy the sheet containing the number and ages of children. Laminate this sheet, and cut the choices apart. Then put them inside the envelope.

3. Copy the page titled "Child Care Expenses" on a sheet of colored paper. Laminate the sheet and attach it to the outside of one of the envelopes.

4. Using the same color paper, copy the sheet containing the child care payments. Laminate this sheet, and cut the choices apart. Then put them inside the envelope.

5. Copy the page titled "Marital Status" on a sheet of colored paper. Laminate the sheet and attach it to the outside of one of the envelopes.

6. Using the same color paper, copy the sheet with the possible choices of married and divorced. Laminate this sheet, and cut the choices apart. Then put them inside the envelope.

7. Copy the page titled "Spouse's Raise" on a sheet of colored paper. Laminate the sheet and attach it to the outside of one of the envelopes.

8. Using the same color paper, copy the sheet with the spouse's raises. Laminate this sheet, and cut the choices apart. Then put them inside the envelope.

9. Using the same color paper you used for the perks and pitfalls, copy the additional perks and pitfalls. Laminate this sheet, and cut the choices apart. Then put them inside the envelope.

10. Copy the You Have a Family: Overview and You Have a Family: Rules sheets for each student in the class.

11. Copy the W-4 sheet for students who may want to make changes, particularly those whose marital status changed.

To Begin the Game

1. Read and discuss the You Have a Family: Overview and You Have a Family: Rules pages.

2. Have students select the number of children and their ages from the envelope.

3. Have students select their marital status of married or divorced from the envelope.

4. If students remain married, have those students select a raise for his or her spouse.

5. Have students select their child care expenses from the envelope. If the child is under the age of 6, they need to have child care for the randomly selected amount. If the child is over the age of 6, you can assume the child will attend school.

6. Discuss the fixed expense sheet. Students will update their post-secondary commitment if there is a change, the number of children and their ages, their marital status, the spouse's raise, and child care expenses.

On the Day Prior to the Last Day of the School Week

1. Have students tally their take-home pay. The taxes and the health insurance premium deductions will be taken out.

2. Have students hand in their binders or folders to a predetermined place.

3. Check each student's take-home pay calculations. If the student is correct, write a paycheck for that amount. If the student is incorrect, mark the mistakes and deduct $100 for each error.

On the Last Day of the School Week

1. Hand back or have students pick up their binders or folders.

2. Post the reminder sheet titled "What You Need to Remember When Dealing with Your Bank Transactions."

3. Students may need to write out a weekly child care check.

4. Have students pay their house payment.

5. Have students select a pitfall or a perk from the envelope.

6. Instruct students to deposit their paycheck, their spouse's wages (don't forget the raise), and any perk they may have received.

7. Have students write out the checks for their bills and any pitfalls they may have received.

8. Instruct students to enter their deposits and checks in their check registers.

9. Encourage students to have their partner check their financial transactions and check register.

10. Have students begin a new time sheet and mark their attendance points. (In general, the time sheet will run from Friday to the following Thursday.)

11. Have students hand in their binder or folder. You can determine how they will be assessed.

Following Weeks

1. Continue with pay stubs, deposits, checks, and perks and pitfalls.

2. During the second week, the bill is two car payments.

3. During the third week, the bill is the utility bill and the cell phone bill (if students decide to keep the cell phone).

4. During the fourth week, the bill is a credit card bill.

5. After the fourth week, the cycle of bills starts over.

You Have a Family: Things to Consider

The financial considerations in this stage include raising children, child care, saving for your child's education, and pets. These activities are to be completed with a partner, preferably of the opposite gender. You may decide to have students complete them any time it is conducive to your classroom schedule.

What's Next? Auction

You can decide at the end of the stage if you are going to hold the auction. Use the same procedure described on page 37.

Name _____ Date _____

You Have a Family: Overview

Congratulations! For the sake of the game, you now have children. The number and age of your children will be randomly selected. Children will definitely change your lifestyle. They will change how you spend your money and your time. Therefore, during the next stage, the game will attempt to recreate some of the changes you may experience when you have children.

The cost of child care will simulate the financial change children can bring. Your child care expenses will be a weekly expense for you if you have children under the age of six. If they are six or older, you can assume they are attending school. The amount of child care you will be expected to pay will be chosen randomly, and you will need to note it on your fixed expense sheet. On a rotating basis, you will also have to pay your house payment, two utility bills, two car payments, and a credit card bill. If you elected to keep your cell phone, you will also have that bill to pay. Furthermore, you cannot forget the perks and pitfalls that you will continue to select on a weekly basis. As you get older and have children, you will find the perks and pitfalls can be more financially beneficial or devastating.

When children are born, it can be stressful for the couple. Instead of just thinking about themselves and their spouse, parents need to think about their children who have unique needs. Parents often make joint decisions regarding their children, but sometimes the parents do not hold similar viewpoints. Compromise is often necessary. During this stage, you and a partner will be asked to consider raising children, child care, saving for your children's education, and pets.

Name _____ Date _____

You Have a Family: Rules

- You are now getting "paid" to show up for class on time. You will earn $250 for daily attendance.

- If you are late for class, you will not earn the $250 for daily attendance. Showing up to work on time is very important and valued by employers.

- If you know you are going to be absent, communicate with your teacher prior to your absence. If you do this, you will not earn your daily attendance points, but you will not lose anything either.

- If you are too ill to come to school, call and leave a message for your teacher prior to the beginning of the school day. You must get in the habit of communicating with your employer if you will not be at work. It is also very important that you personally call in unless you are absolutely not able to call in yourself. If you do not call in on time, this will result in a loss of **$1,000.** Yes, that is steep, but not calling in when you are not able to work is a good way to lose a job.

- If you have completed post-secondary schooling during the first three stages, your hard work and diligence will pay off. You will now be paid double the daily attendance points.

- If you have not completed your post-secondary schooling at the beginning of this stage, you need to decide if you are going to pursue post-secondary training. If you do pursue post-secondary training (which you will declare on the Post-Secondary Commitment Sheet), you will need to donate a considerable amount of time and energy to your studies. Therefore, during the stage of your post-secondary training, you will earn half as much for attendance points. You may quit post-secondary training at any time, but you will lose all that you have invested. You may only declare you are going to pursue post-secondary training at the start of each stage.

- You will earn money for completing quality work. An assignment in the "A" or "B" range is worth $800.

Name _____ Date _____

- You may be asked to complete projects, but generally a project requires more time and effort. Your teacher will differentiate between an assignment and a project. Therefore, a project in the "A" range is worth $1,750, and a project in the "B" range is worth $1,500.

- Exemplary classroom participation, behavior, and volunteer work may also earn you points. The point values to be earned are left to the discretion of your teacher.

- Poor behavior warranting disciplinary actions will result in a $2,000 fine. Inappropriate behavior will not be tolerated at a place of employment.

Organization

- Keep a current time sheet and update it daily. Your time sheet will document positive and negative dollar values earned. If you earn negative dollar values, you should have your teacher initial it on your time sheet.

- Keep your current time sheet and your current rule sheet in your folder or binder. In addition, keep all of your checks, deposit tickets, and check registers in your binder or folder. If any other material is found, you will pay a $50 penalty to your teacher.

- The assignment and project points you earn should be documented on the day they are handed back.

- If you are absent on the day assignment or project points are awarded, it is your responsibility to ask your teacher for the points you missed on the day you return. If you do not ask that day, it is up to your teacher whether or not the points will be awarded.

- Volunteer points and other miscellaneous points you earn should only be written down on the day they are earned.

- Tally your time sheet one day prior to the last day of the week so your teacher can use it to write out a check.

- If your teacher cannot easily find your time sheet, or you fail to put it in your binder or folder, you will not be paid for that pay period.

Name _____ Date _____

- If you have mistakes on your time sheet, you will lose $100 for each mistake. If you are found to be dishonest, you will lose everything!

Dealing with Your Financial Transactions

- Since you are a parent, you are required to pay bills every week. For this stage, your bills include the following: housing, two car payments, two utility bills, cell phone bill (if you chose to keep the cell phone), and a credit card bill. Pay your housing bill the first week, your two auto bills the second week, your utility bills and cell phone bill (if applicable) the third week, and your credit card bill the fourth week. Then repeat the process. Since you are married and have a family, you have a fixed housing expense and two car payments. These are the same fixed expenses as you had in the last stage. The utility bills and credit card bill will change as you draw a different amount from the provided envelope each time. The cell phone bill, if you decide it is a necessity, will continue to be drawn the week you pay your utility bill.

- Positive and negative events occur that are beyond your control. At the end of each week, draw a pitfall or a perk from the provided envelope. A pitfall is something you need to write out a check for, and a perk is a deposit. On the last day of the week, you will write a check for your bill and the pitfall. If a specific payee is not provided, you need to come up with an appropriate one. Use the phone book as a reference.

- On the last day of the week, you will write a deposit ticket for your paycheck, your spouse's paycheck, and any perk you may have received. Combine all of your deposits on one ticket.

- With the checks and deposit tickets you have written out, accurately and completely fill in the check register.

- Keeping accurate financial records, writing out checks, and filling in deposit tickets are very important. You can easily get yourself in financial trouble by making just a few mistakes.

- Your teacher will inform you how the checks, deposits, and check register will be graded.

Name _____ Date _____

Divorce

- Since the divorce rate in the United States is approximately 51%, at the beginning of the stage, you will randomly select if you will remain married or become divorced.

- If you get divorced, you will no longer receive your spouse's wages. However, you will not have to pay two car payments. You will pay one. The other bills will remain the same.

Child Care

- At the beginning of the stage, you will randomly select the number and age of your children.

- Since 4 out of 5 families are dual-income families, you will need to consider having child care outside of the home. You will randomly select the hourly rate and the number of hours you will need child care.

- You will need to write out a weekly check for the child care bill. For every child under the age of 5, you will need to pay weekly child care bills. For the children between the ages of 5–12, you may need to pay for child care before and after school.

Spouse's Income

You and your spouse both contribute to the family's finances. As you each gain more experience and seniority at your job, you are each eligible for earning a raise. You will randomly select if your spouse receives a raise, and if so, how much. Make sure your fixed expense sheet and weekly bank transactions reflect this change. If you are divorced, you do not have to bother selecting a slip because you no longer have a spouse's income affecting your finances. You will randomly select your spouse's weekly income from the provided envelope.

Name _____ Date _____

Taxes

Taxes are a reality when you work. You cannot get out of paying them. You will need to continue to calculate and deduct from your weekly gross pay the tax contributions for FICA and Medicare, using the provided percentages on the time sheet.

- Use the provided federal income tax forms, your marital status (remember, you are married now), and the withholding allowance to calculate your federal income tax withholding to deduct from your weekly gross pay.

- If you want to change your withholding allowance to reflect your children as dependents, you will need to complete a new W-4.

- Your teacher will give you instructions if you are to deduct state income tax contributions.

Health Insurance

Health insurance is extremely important. Health expenses are very expensive, and buying your own health insurance policy is also very expensive. However, it is not wise to live without health insurance. Therefore, most employers offer health insurance as a benefit, but most employees need to pay a portion of the premium. Select your health insurance premium contribution at the beginning of the stage, and you will deduct it from your weekly pay.

Number and Age of Children

3 children—ages 6, 4, and 3	2 children—ages 9 and 7
2 children—ages 3 and 5	1 child—age 3
1 child—age 5	2 children—ages 10 and 4
2 children—ages 6 and 1	1 child—age 4
2 children—ages 8 and 10	1 child—age 3 months
4 children—ages 2, 4, 6, and 7	No children
3 children—ages 2, 6, and 8	2 children—ages 9 and 6
3 children—ages 3, 5 and 8	No children
1 child—age 1 month	1 child—age 9 month
3 children—ages 7, 4, and 1	2 children—ages 8 and 4

Child Care Expenses

$2.50 per hour per child 42 hours per week	$1.75 per hour per child 22 hours per week
$100.00 per week per child	Grandma babysits for free
$3.50 per hour per child 40 hours per week	$3.70 per hour per child 40 hours per week
$4.10 per hour per child 30 hours per week	$2.95 per hour per child 43 hours per week
$3.50 per hour per child 25 hours per week	$3.00 per hour per child 35 hours per week
$3.75 per hour per child 33 hours per week	$135.00 per week per child
$95.00 per week per child	$155.00 per week per child
$2.75 per hour per child 32 hours per week	$5.50 per hour per child 40 hours per week
$4.75 per hour per child 15 hours per week	$3.75 per hour per child 45 hours per week
$175 per week per child	$95.00 per week per child

Spouse's Raise

No raise	No raise
No raise	No raise
No raise	No raise
No raise	No raise
Spouse loses job	Spouse gets a raise of $300 per paycheck
Spouse gets a raise of $50 per paycheck	Spouse gets a raise of $70 per paycheck
Spouse gets a new job paying $850 per paycheck	Spouse gets a raise of $30 per paycheck
Spouse gets a raise of $150 per paycheck	Spouse gets a new job paying $1,235 per paycheck
Spouse gets a new job paying $960 per paycheck	Spouse gets a new job paying $550 per paycheck
Spouse gets a new job paying $1,200 per paycheck	Spouse gets a raise of $20 per paycheck

Marital Status

Married	Married
Married	Married
Married	Married
Married	Married
Married	Married
Divorced	Divorced
Divorced	Divorced
Divorced	Divorced
Divorced	Divorced
Divorced	Divorced

Additional Perks

$5,000.00 inheritance	$2,000.00 bonus at work
$2,100.00 sold old car	$452.50 rummage sale profit
$200.00 sold old computer	$900.00 sold CD collection
$3,500.00 bonus at work	$2,500.00 Certificate of Deposit matured
$550.00 seasonal employment	$1,000.00 won an award
$600.00 won a raffle	$10,000.00 inheritance
$450.00 sold a painting	$400.00 worked on a friend's car
$200.00 helped a friend move	$1,673.33 stock dividends
$2,932.89 stock dividends	$783.32 second job's earnings
$2,500.00 bonus at work	$ 893.32 sold an appliance

Additional Pitfalls

$2,300.00 child's tuition	$3,003.32 new furniture
$25.00 school registration	$350.00 driver's education registration
$28.90 child's book order	$6,127.32 child needs braces
$93.32 child's unexpected cell phone bill	$456.32 took family to a water park
$98.32 child's new shoes	$75.00 entry fee for child's enrichment activities
$25.00 Little League fundraiser	$6,500.00 took family on vacation
$500.00 camp fee	$1,200.00 laptop computer
$5,200.00 swimming pool	$326.32 trampoline
$3,200.00 4-wheeler	$145.00 new sports equipment
$320.89 children's pictures	$345.00 music equipment

Name _____   Date _____

Raising Your Children

How many times have you said to yourself, "When I become a parent, I will
never . . . "? If you are like most people, you have said that before, and
probably more than once. Everyone has an opinion about how to raise
children. This is evident by the many magazines dedicated to parenting, the
frequent news stories and television shows to improve parenting skills, and
even suggestions offered by a total stranger in the grocery store. However,
when you are a parent, you will have to decide how you are going to raise
your child (or children). In a two-parent home, you and your spouse will have
to collaborate to make decisions jointly. Every day a parent must make many
decisions regarding his or her children, so the questions asked here are just
the tip of the "parental iceberg." For this exercise, you will be working with a
partner to answer the questions that follow. Each of you should use a
different color ink to differentiate your answers.

Name _____   Date _____

Eating

1. Your child is a picky eater and will often refuse to eat what has been made. How do you handle this situation?

2. Your child likes to snack throughout the day. Is this a problem? Explain.

3. At the age of two, your child recognizes the "Golden Arches." Is fast food something that is acceptable, and if so, how much? Explain.

Name _____ Date _____

4. What type of snacks would you have in the house for a five-year-old child? Explain the choices you would provide.

5. You like to go to fancy restaurants, but your toddler has trouble sitting quietly and not disturbing you and the other patrons in the restaurant. How do you handle the situation?

Name _____ Date _____

Sleeping

1. Is it okay for your child to sleep in your bed with you? Explain.

2. Your baby does not sleep through the night. In fact, she is up several times a night. What do you do?

3. When should children stop taking naps? Explain.

4. Your toddler is often up at night. She seems to just want the reassurance you are there. How do you respond?

Name _____ Date _____

Discipline

1. Your two-year-old son just dumped over a box of cereal right after you told him to be careful. How do you react? Explain.

2. Your six-year-old son just told you in a very "sassy" tone that he is not going to do what you just asked him to. How do you react? Explain.

3. Your eight-year-old daughter didn't give you a note from her teacher saying that she failed a spelling test. How do you respond?

4. Your four-year-old daughter just told a stranger at the grocery store that she is "fat." How do you react?

Name _____ Date _____

School and Activities

1. Is preschool really necessary? Explain.

2. You are considering taking your infant to a program for music enrichment. What do you decide and why? Explain.

3. Do you believe your children should get their education through the public or private school system? Explain.

4. Do you think your child should be involved in sports and clubs after school? If so, which ones and how many?

Name _____ Date _____

Friends

1. Your child has a friend you feel is a bad influence. What do you do?

2. Your child is getting bullied by kids at school. How do you react?

3. Your nine-year-old son has asked for a cell phone. Do you buy him one? Why or why not?

4. Your eleven-year-old daughter was 30 minutes late getting home from a friend's house. How do you handle the situation?

Name _____ Date _____

Child Care

If you have a child, child care is a major decision you will need to make. There are diverse opinions on how child care should be handled. With your partner, discuss the questions listed below and write your responses with different color ink to differentiate your opinions.

1. After a child is born, should one person quit his or her job and stay home with the infant? If so, who? Why did you select that person? If no, why not?

2. If you have to find child care outside the home, list four different options you might consider.

3. What type of child care would be your first choice? Why?

Name _____ Date _____

4. Name five different things that you feel are important to look for when considering a child care provider. List them below.

5. Find the name of four different day care centers in your area. Call one and find out the cost for an infant under the age of one, a three-year-old child, and before- and after-school care for a school-age child. Report your findings below.

6. How often do you feel you should get a babysitter at night to allow you and your spouse to go out together? Explain.

Name _____ Date _____

7. When do you think you will want to leave your children for a vacation in which you will be gone for one week? Why do you feel this way?

8. What is the typical cost to get a babysitter at night for two children? (You may have to ask someone if you do not know.)

9. You came home earlier than you expected, and the children were supposed to be in bed. However, all of the children are up and the house is in utter chaos. How do you handle it?

Name _____ Date _____

Saving for Your Child's Education

There will probably come a time in your life when you will ask yourself, "How am I going to pay for my child's education?" Maybe you will have thought about it before your first child is born, and maybe you won't think about it until they enter high school. On average, most people only have around $10,000 saved by the time their child is ready to go to college. Unfortunately, this is well below what it will cost. As you will find out, there are many different ways you can save for an education. The question is, how soon will you start?

1. Do some research and find the projected tuition cost (20 years from now) for a four-year college and for a two-year college. Write your response below.

2. When should you start saving for your child's education? Explain.

3. Look on the Internet and list three ways you can start saving money for your child's education.

4. What are some things you can do if you don't have enough money to pay for your child's college education? List some ideas below.

Name _____ Date _____

Pets

Pet ownership is very common, but there are many aspects about pet ownership that you need to consider before you bring a pet home. Prior to getting a pet, you may need to consider the following:

1. What are three positive effects that can result from owning a pet? List them below.

2. What are three negative effects that can result from owning a pet? List them below.

3. Name ten different types of pet you may be able to own if you lived in an apartment in a city. List them below.

4. Name ten different types of pets you could own if you have a home in a rural area. List them below.

Name _____ Date _____

5. Using the pets listed in questions 3 and 4, which pet would you chose? Why did you choose that pet? (If you are doing this with a partner, differentiate using different color ink.)

6. A pet is generally something a whole family needs to agree on, so if you did not agree in the previous question with your partner, how will you compromise?

7. When you are looking for a pet, name four characteristics you would desire in this type of pet. List them below.

8. If you were to buy this pet, determine the average cost. Name your source.

Name _____ Date _____

9. List the needed pet supplies for this pet. Determine an approximate cost for each item. Total your pet supply expenses. Name your source.

10. What will the pet eat? About how much food will the pet need for one week? About how much will it cost to feed the animal for one week? One month? One year?

11. What type of ongoing care will the pet need? What is the cost for this ongoing care? Name your source.

Answer Key

Renting

1. newspaper, Internet, friends, family

2. Answers will vary. Acceptable answers could be location, cost, space, number of rooms, appliances included, and so forth.

3. Answers will vary. Possible advantages: includes utilities, it may be furnished, renter not responsible for overall maintenance, not responsible for property taxes, financial responsibility limited to rent and security deposit, and so forth. Possible disadvantages: you do not own it, you are not building equity, limited privacy, unable to make changes without permission, possible eviction, and so forth.

4. Answers will vary, but may include such things as heat, water, appliances, garage, and so forth.

5. Answers will vary, but may include security deposit, electricity, cable, and telephone.

6. Answers will vary, but may include various types of furniture, items for kitchen, or things for the bathroom. The cost could be found on the web sites of different stores.

7–8. Finding an apartment or house to rent can be done by looking in the newspaper or online.

9–10. amount of rent divided by 40

Purchasing a Car

1. Answers will vary, but may include questions such as the following: What kind of warranty does the car have? How many miles per gallon does the car get? What safety features are included?

2. Answers will vary, but may include questions such as, How many miles are on it? What year is it? Why are you selling your car? Was the car ever in an accident?

3. bank, credit union, car dealership

4–5. Interest rates can be found by looking on a bank's web site under loans.

6. Car description will vary.

7. Use an auto loan calculator found on the Internet.

8. Auto insurance companies can be found on the Internet or in a phone book.

9. Auto insurance requirements vary by state. This information can be obtained from a local insurance office or on the Internet.

10. Bodily injury insurance helps pay for an injured person's medical expenses and lost wages if you're at fault in a car accident.

11. Collision insurance helps you pay for damage to your own car if your car hits another vehicle or object.

12. Answers will vary, but may include age, if you are married, if you have had an accident before, if you live in the city or the country, how far you drive to work or school, and so forth.

Opening a Checking Account

1. identification such as a driver's license, social security card, money to deposit in the account

2. Direct deposit is when your place of employment puts your paycheck directly into your savings or checking account.

3. a bank or a credit union

4. Answers will vary, but may include factors such as whether or not they are insured, the types of accounts they have, and the location and history of the bank.

5. Students should look at financial institutions in their area and research them.

6. ask friends and family, visit the bank personally, use the Internet

7. Answers will vary.

Luxury Item

1. Answers will vary, but may include items such as a car stereo system, a home entertainment system, or a big-screen television.

2. To find the costs of items, students can look on the Internet or in newspaper ads.

3–6.   Answers will vary depending on the student's luxury item.

Comparing Credit Cards

Answers will fluctuate. The teacher should visit a credit card comparison site for current information.

Taxes

1. $96; $123; $17; $177
2. $566.26; $713.99; $332.65; $411.31
3. $60.95; $119.04; $26.60
4. $12.93; $8.44; $27.43

Your Food Allowance

Answers will vary depending on grocery allotment and student choices.

Furnishing a Place to Live

Answers will vary depending on furnishing allotment and student choices.

Entertainment Allowance

Answers will vary depending on students' activities.

Buying Appliances

1.   Answers will vary, but may include a refrigerator, an oven, a washer, a dryer, a dishwasher, a microwave, a TV, and so forth.
2.   Answers will vary, but may include the warranty, size, cost, special features, and so forth.
3.   Prices and sales can be found on the Internet or in newspapers or flyers.
4.   The features will be the primary difference.
5–8.   Answers will vary.

Savings

1.   Answers will vary, but may include large purchases, college, retirement, or emergencies.
2.   Answers will vary, but may include that a person could be in debt, fails to follow a budget, and buys things spontaneously.

3.   A *need* is something that could be hard to live without. A *want* is something you can live without.
4.   Answers will vary, but may include getting a financial advisor, opening a savings account or a retirement account, and having money deposited directly into savings.
5.   Answers will vary, but may include savings accounts, stocks and bonds, and certificates of deposit.
6.   Answers will vary, but may include spouse, family member, or a financial advisor.

Health Insurance

Answers will vary depending on where you receive services.

Are Men and Women Really That Different?

Answers will vary.

Buying a House

1.   Answers will vary.
2.   Home descriptions will vary.
3. $20,000; $50,000; answers will vary
4.   Answers will vary depending on current interest rates. Students can find interest rates online, or they can call a local financial institution.
5.   cost of home × .20 or .30
6.   Answers will vary.
7.   annual property tax divided by 12

Celebrations

Answers will vary.

Having a Baby

1.   A newborn needs to be changed approximately every 2 hours, so a minimum of 12 diapers per day will be used, and subsequently, 360 diapers a month. The cost varies by brand. A typical package of approximately 100 diapers has a price range between $20–$30, but the student should check local prices.

2. Answers will vary, but may include a car seat, crib, changing table, baby monitor, stroller, and a bouncy seat.

3. Answers will vary. A one-month-old may wake up every 2 hours, or may sleep through the night. A one-year-old may wake up several times a night, once a night, or may sleep through the night.

4. Students can search the Internet for the cost of formula, and ask a parent or friend how long a can of formula will last. The total cost will vary depending on the type of formula, but formula costs approximately $1,500 a year, depending on the brand.

5. helps the baby through immunity, is free, can be more convenient because breast milk is always available

6. A newborn typically eats every 2–3 hours.

7. Doctor visits may vary, but a typical schedule is 2 weeks, 1 month, 3 months, 6 months, 9 months, 1 year, 15 months, 18 months, 2 years, and then annually.

8. Answers will vary. According to The Agency for Healthcare Research and Quality, the average cost of a vaginal delivery with no complication is $6,200, and a C-section with no complications is $11,500, but costs vary depending on location and doctor.

9. Jaundice is a yellowish tint to the skin and the whites of the eyes, caused by high levels of the chemical bilirubin. The treatment depends on the cause.

10. SIDS is Sudden Infant Death Syndrome. This is when an infant suddenly stops breathing and dies. To help reduce the risk of SIDS, you should place your baby on his or her back to sleep, and not put any pillows, blankets, or stuffed animals in the crib. Answers may vary, as there are other factors that are thought to help reduce the risk of SIDS.

11. when the baby is acting abnormally, crying uncontrollably, running a fever, or lethargic

12. A pediatrician is a doctor who cares for small children. When choosing a pediatrician, answers may vary, but could include recommendations from family or friends, and researching and interviewing the physician.

Going on Vacation

1. Answers will vary, but may include talking to spouse or children, looking at the Internet or other advertising material, and consulting a travel agent.

2. Answers will vary. Students can search the Internet for a place they want to visit, look at hotels in cities where they may want to stay, or they can speak to a travel agent.

3. Answers may vary, but may include taking along lunches or staying at hotels that offer continental breakfast, looking for discounts, or finding activities with minimal or no entrance fee.

4. Answers may vary. Answers may include using the Internet to search for places to visit and the costs for each, booking hotels in advance to get a discount, or getting an estimate for the vacation and putting money away in advance.

5. Answers will vary based on local prices.

6. Answers will vary.

Raising Your Children

Answers will vary.

Child Care

1. Answers will vary.

2. in-home babysitter, family, day care, nanny, preschool

3. Answers will vary.

4. Answers will vary, but may include reputation, safety, location, cost, activities, and so forth.

5. Students can find day care centers in a phone book. Have students explain to the person they speaking with that they are doing this for an assignment.

6–9. Answers will vary.

Saving for Your Child's Education

1. Current estimates state that a private college may be as much as $300,000.

2. No specific answer, but many believe as soon as the child is born.

3. section 529 plans, education saving accounts, investments

4. financial aid, loans

Pets

1. Answers will vary, but may include companionship, learning experience, entertainment, and protection.

2. Answers will vary, but may include that it takes time, costs money, and tough decisions may have to be made (such as putting it to sleep or giving it up).

3. Answers will vary, but may include dog, cat, rat, hamster, snake, fish, turtle, guinea pig, bird, and so forth.

4. Answers will vary, but may include dog, cat, rat, hamster, snake, fish, turtle, guinea pig, bird, cow, horse, pig, goat, sheep, and so forth.

5–11. Answers will vary depending on pet.

WALCH EDUCATION
extending and enhancing learning

Let's stay in touch!

Thank you for purchasing these Walch Education materials. Now, we d like to support you in your role as an educator. **Register now** and we'll provide you with updates on related publications, online resources, and more. You can register online at www.walch.com/newsletter, or fill out this form and fax or mail it to us.

Name _____ Date _____

School name _____

School address_____

City _____ State _____ Zip _____

Phone number (home) _____ (school) _____

E-mail _____

Grade level(s) taught _____ Subject area(s) _____

Where did you purchase this publication? _____

When do you primarily purchase supplemental materials? _____

What moneys were used to purchase this publication?

[   ] School supplemental budget

[   ] Federal/state funding

[   ] Personal

[   ] Please sign me up for Walch Education's free quarterly e-newsletter, *Education Connection*.

[   ] Please notify me regarding free *Teachable Moments* downloads.

[   ] Yes, you may use my comments in upcoming communications.

COMMENTS _____

_____

_____

_____

Please FAX this completed form to 888-991-5755, or mail it to:
Customer Service, Walch Education, 40 Walch Drive, Portland, ME 04103